ACTIVE LEARNING

DINOSAURS
&OTHER PREHISTORIC CREATURES

Senior Editors Rebecca Fry,
Satu Hämeenaho-Fox
Editor Sarah Carpenter
US Senior Editor Kayla Dugger
US Executive Editor Lori Cates Hand
Art Editor Jessica Tapolcai
Project Art Editors Laura Gardner Design Studio,
Mark Lloyd, Anna Scully
Managing Editor Carine Tracanelli
Managing Art Editor Anna Hall
Jacket Designer Stephanie Cheng Hui Tan
Jacket Design Development Manager
Sophia MTT
Senior Jackets Coordinator
Priyanka Sharma Saddi
Senior Production Editor Andy Hilliard
Senior Production Controller Poppy David
Art Director Karen Self
Publisher Andrew Macintyre
Publishing Director Jonathan Metcalf

Illustrators Mark Ruffle, Edwood Burn,
John Haslam Illustration, Vacharin Vacharopast

First American Edition, 2023
Published in the United States by DK Publishing
1745 Broadway, 20th Floor, New York, NY 10019

A catalog record for this book
is available from the Library of Congress.
ISBN 978-0-7440-8150-3

Printed and bound in China

For the curious
www.dk.com

MIX
Paper | Supporting
responsible forestry
FSC™ C018179

This book was made with Forest
Stewardship Council™ certified
paper—one small step in DK's
commitment to a sustainable future.
For more information go to
www.dk.com/our-green-pledge

THE AUTHOR AND CONSULTANT

Lizzie Munsey edits and writes books for children.
She has worked in publishing for more than a decade
and has contributed to scores of books on natural
history, including DK's *Extraordinary Dinosaurs* and
Dinosaur Ultimate Handbook. Her favorite dinosaur
is *Parasaurolophus*. Lizzie lives in Gloucestershire,
England, with her two children, two cats, and a various
number of chickens.

Riley Black, our consultant on this book, is author of the
two best-selling books—*The Last Days of the Dinosaurs*
and *Skeleton Keys*—plus many other fossiliferous books.
She is a regular science writer for *National Geographic*,
The Smithsonian, *Nature*, *Science*, and *Scientific American*.
When not writing about fossils, Riley joins museum and
university field teams to search for new fossils across
the American Southwest. She has also appeared in
documentaries such as NOVA's *Alaskan Dinosaurs*.

CONTENTS

CHECK WHEN COMPLETED!

WHAT IS A DINOSAUR?

Dinosaurs thrived on Earth for more than 167 million years and continue to live today as modern birds. This diverse and successful group of land reptiles came in all shapes and sizes—some were gigantic herbivores that walked on four sturdy legs, while others were tiny, two-legged carnivores.

The reptile family

Dinosaurs were part of the reptile family but were different in many ways from lizards and snakes—some had feathers, as well as scaly skin. They belonged to a group of reptiles called archosaurs. This group also included nondinosaurs—flying reptiles called pterosaurs and early members of the crocodile family.

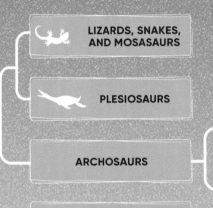

- LIZARDS, SNAKES, AND MOSASAURS
- PLESIOSAURS
- ARCHOSAURS
  - CROCODYLOMORPHS
  - PTEROSAURS
  - DINOSAURS AND BIRDS
- ICHTHYOSAURS
- TURTLES AND TORTOISES

REPTILES

a

b

c

d

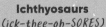
WRITE IT!

MATCH THE CREATURES!

Here are some nondinosaur reptiles that lived alongside the dinosaurs during the Mesozoic Era. Use their descriptions to help you work out which is which, then add the correct letter.

Ichthyosaurs
(ick-thee-oh-SORES)
These marine reptiles had big eyes and looked similar to today's dolphins.

Plesiosaurs
(PLEA-see-oh-sores)
These were long-necked, water-living reptiles with flippers.

Pterosaurs
(TER-oh-sores)
These flying reptiles had wings made of stretched skin attached to their back legs.

Crocodylomorphs
(CROC-oh-DIL-oh-morfs)
These reptiles were the ancestors of our modern crocodiles and alligators.

WHOSE LEGS?

Dinosaurs had legs that were positioned differently from those of other reptiles. Use the descriptions to help you work out which stance belongs to each type of reptile, then draw lines to connect the pairs.

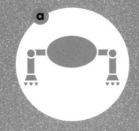
a

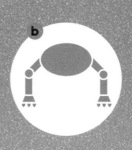
b

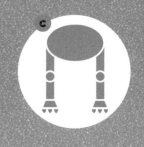
c

MATCH IT!

Dinosaur
The legs of dinosaurs were tucked underneath their bodies. This allowed them to walk quickly and some to stand upright.

Lizard
Lizard limbs sprawl outward, sticking out from either side of their bodies. They can move fast, but not for long.

Crocodile
Many species in the crocodile family have limbs with bent joints. They can briefly lift their bodies off the ground.

IS IT A DINOSAUR?

Look at these animals and read their descriptions, then answer the questions in the flow chart below to work out if they are dinosaurs or not.
Hint: Dinosaurs lived on land.

Pterodactylus (ter-oh-DACK-til-us)
This flying reptile had wings made of stretched skin and ate fish and clams.

☐ Yes ☐ No

Hypsilophodon (HIP-sih-LOAF-oh-don)
This small, speedy herbivore ran on two legs through the undergrowth.

☐ Yes ☐ No

Are its legs tucked under its body?

NO   YES

Does it have scales or feathers?

NO   YES

NOT A DINOSAUR   IT'S A DINOSAUR

Deinosuchus (DIE-no-SOO-kuss)
This relative of today's alligators could grow to up to 39 feet (12 m) long.

☐ Yes ☐ No

Sauroposeidon (SORE-oh-pos-i-den)
Longer than four buses, this herbivore stomped around Cretaceous forests.

☐ Yes ☐ No

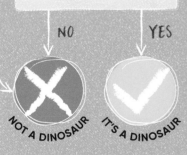
CHECK IT!

Stenopterygius (sten-OP-terr-IDGE-ee-us)
This reptile's torpedo-shaped body helped it speed through Jurassic seas.

☐ Yes ☐ No

Archelon (ARCH-eh-lon)
This giant sea turtle had a leathery shell and wide flippers for swimming.

☐ Yes ☐ No

5

PALEONTOLOGY

Paleontology is the study of prehistoric life, including dinosaurs. As we can't turn back time to see the plants and animals from millions of years ago, paleontologists have to be detectives. They piece together the fossil evidence and try to deduce what dinosaurs looked like and how they lived. New fossils are found all the time, so theories about dinosaurs change.

IN 1811, **MARY ANNING** FOUND AN **ICHTHYOSAUR SKELETON** WHEN SHE WAS ONLY **12.**

COMPLETE THE SKELETON

It's very unusual to find a complete skeleton. To work out what a dinosaur looked like, paleontologists often piece together fossils from different dig sites or compare the bones with existing animal skeletons. This dinosaur has five bones missing. Find them on these pages and draw them in the right place.

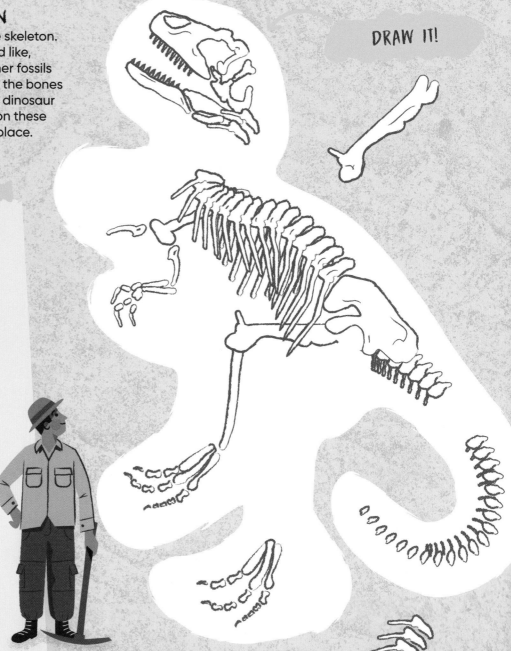

DRAW IT!

STUDY THE BONES

Imagine that you are the paleontologist who found this dinosaur skeleton. Look at its bones and teeth, then answer the following questions:

a How many legs do you think it walked on?

☐ Two
☐ Four

b What shape are its teeth?

☐ Long and sharp
☐ Round with flat tops

c What do you think it ate?

☐ Plants
☐ Other dinosaurs

The first dino fossils

Indigenous Peoples had dug up and understood dinosaur bones long before scientists ever did. Then, in 1842, scientist Richard Owen studied some of the earliest fossil bones found in the UK. He identified a new group of giant, extinct reptiles that he called "dinosaurs."

Megalosaurus
(MEG-ah-LOSS-er-oss)
In 1676, a mysterious bone was found in a quarry, which was later identified as part of the thigh bone of this giant Jurassic carnivore.

Hylaeosaurus
(high-LEE-o-SORE-us)
In 1832, over 50 bones were found in a slab of quarry rock. When pieced together, they revealed this armored reptile from the Early Cretaceous.

Iguanodon
(ig-GWAH-no-don)
In 1822, amateur fossil hunter Mary Mantell found a collection of teeth beside a road. They turned out to be from this giant Cretaceous herbivore.

NAME THAT DINOSAUR

Many scientific names for dinosaurs are from Latin, Greek, or a mixture of the two languages. The names often describe a dinosaur's features. Look at the English translations of these dinosaurs' names in the word box, then write the correct one under each dinosaur.

> Chicken mimic
> Parrot lizard
> Heavy claw
> Spiked lizard
> Three-horned face

KENTROSAURUS

TRICERATOPS

a ....
....

b ....
....

WRITE IT!

BARYONYX

GALLIMIMUS

PSITTACOSAURUS

c ....
....

d ....
....

e ....
....

DIGGING UP DINOSAURS

Paleontologists study fossils to learn about ancient life. However, before they can do that, they must find the fossils and dig them up. Excavating fossils can be a difficult and slow process. It must be done carefully to avoid damaging these precious records of the past.

Used for holding fragile fossils together until they can be studied

Paleontologists' tools
Paleontologists use a range of tools to carefully remove fossils from the ground:

Straight-headed hammer
The wedge-shaped side of this hammer can be used to split rocks open.

Lump hammer and chisel
A square-headed lump hammer is used to drive a chisel into the rock. Together, they can be used to clear areas of rock away from around a fossil.

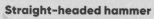

Paintbrushes
Brushes of different sizes are used to gently sweep dust and debris away from the fossil as it is uncovered.

Glue
Fossils can be fragile. To stop them from crumbling, they are painted with glue and then wrapped in plaster.

DRAW THE TOOLS
Read the information in the tools panel to help you figure out which objects are missing here. Then draw them in.

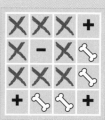

A tool for gently removing small amounts of debris

LOCATE THE FOSSILS
Work out where the fossils are hidden at this dig site. They must be next to a plus sign (+) but can't be next to a minus sign (–). The examples below show you how to reveal the squares where the fossils lie.

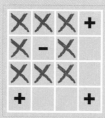

1. Start by making crosses in all the squares touching a "–." Include any diagonal squares.

2. Draw bones in all remaining squares, but only if they are next to a plus "+" sign.

THE WORD **FOSSIL** COMES FROM LATIN **AND MEANS "DUG UP!"**

DRAW IT!

A tool for splitting rocks apart

Two tools, used together, for finely chipping away sections of rock

HOW DO FOSSILS FORM?

The remains of living things can become fossils, in a process called fossilization. They undergo chemical changes, as minerals replace some (but usually not all) of the original animal. Fossilization can take millions of years and only occurs in exactly the right circumstances—the remains must have been buried under layers of sediment in order to be preserved.

THE OLDEST **FOSSILS** FOUND SO FAR ARE TINY ORGANISMS NEARLY **3.5 BILLION** YEARS OLD.

 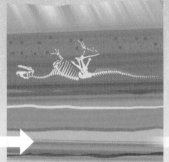 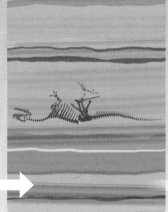 

1 Death
An animal dies in a place where sediment is being deposited, like near a river, lake, or volcano. This dead dinosaur is lying in mud and will be covered by ash from a volcano.

2 Burial
The soft parts of the animal's body rot away, leaving only bones. Over time, more layers of sediment build up over the bones, and pressure turns the layers into solid rock.

3 Turn to stone
Minerals from the ground gradually seep into the animal's bones and harden into rock. The skeleton has now become a fossil inside a layer of rock.

4 Excavation
Eventually, the layers of rock above the fossil are eroded—worn away by the wind and rain. The fossil is exposed and can be excavated by a paleontologist.

FIND THE FOSSIL NAME
The most common fossils are the shells of marine creatures that died and sank quickly into the seabed. Replace each number with a letter of the alphabet (1 = a, 2 = b, 3 = c, and so on) to find the name of this fossilized animal.

1 13 13 15 14 9 20 5

START HERE!

_ _ _ _ _ _ _ _

Sedimentary rock
Sandstone is one type of this rock, formed from sandy layers.

BURY THE DINO BONES

The dinosaur below died a long time ago and was buried beneath many layers of sediment, which have turned to stone. Each rock layer tells paleontologists about the climate, landscape, and events at the time. For example, volcanic ash turns to tuff, mud turns to mudstone, and clay turns to shale. Draw some more fossils below, then color the rock layers in any order.

Coloring key

- Tuff
- Sandstone
- Mudstone
- Shale

COLOR IT!

WHAT WENT WRONG?

Most ancient lifeforms have not been preserved—without the right conditions, they disappear. Read the descriptions, then write the reason why each animal won't become a fossil.

Ocean waves

No sediment

Nothing left

a ....
This dead dinosaur is being eaten by a pack of carnivores. Between them all, they completely devour the whole carcass.

b ....
This animal has died but stays uncovered by any more layers of sand, mud, or ash, so it cannot become a fossil.

c ....
This sea creature has died where there are strong currents. Its shell will be slowly worn away instead of being preserved.

TRAP THE CREATURES

Amber forms when sticky tree sap hardens and solidifies. If a small creature gets stuck in the sap, it is preserved for eternity. Pieces of amber come in all shapes and sizes. Color these creatures, then draw amber to encase them, like the insect below.

INSECT IN AMBER

COLOR IT!

FOSSILS

Fossils are the preserved remains or traces of ancient life. Some are tiny and can only be seen under a microscope, while others are the gigantic bones of colossal dinosaurs. Paleontologists study fossils to try to learn what ancient animals looked like and how they might have lived.

Types of fossils

There are several different types of fossils. Some are the preserved remains of actual body parts; others show us how animals once behaved. Fossil hunters often draw sketches of their "finds"—here are a few.

Skull of a small carnivorous dinosaur from the Jurassic

Body fossil
This is the actual remains of an animal or plant. Usually, only hard parts are fossilized, such as the bones and teeth of an animal or the trunk of a tree.

Cast of a trilobite (a marine animal)

Mold and cast
If an animal dies and rots away, the space can be filled with minerals, creating a cast fossil (copy). When the cast is removed, its imprint is called a mold fossil.

Dinosaur tracks are one of the most common trace fossils.

Trace fossil
These fossils are the fossilized "traces" of animals rather than body parts. They include footprints, nests, eggs, and poop.

This baby mammoth was preserved in ice.

Exceptional preservation
In rare cases, a body fossil is found with some soft tissues (skin or body organs) still present. This can occur when an animal is trapped and dies in ice, tar, peat, or tree sap.

WRITE IT!

a ....

b ....

c ....

d ....

e ....

f ....

Copy of an ammonite
This marine creature died and was buried. Minerals then created a copy of it.

Dinosaur egg
If egg shells are found, they tell scientists about the nurturing habits of dinosaurs.

Megalodon tooth
Many fossilized teeth of this giant extinct shark have been found around the world.

Ammonite imprint
When the ammonite copy above was dug out, it left an impression in the rock.

Dinosaur poop
Sometimes, poop becomes fossilized. It tells scientists about a dinosaur's diet.

Petrified tree stump
If a tree is buried under the right conditions, over time its trunk can be fossilized.

WHICH TYPE?
Read the Types of fossils panel, then look at the labels on this tray. Decide if they are **body**, **cast**, **mold**, or **trace** fossils, then write the type above each fossil.

GEOLOGICAL TIMELINE

Earth has existed for almost 4.6 billion years. To help us keep track of what happened when, we divide the planet's history into sections, known as geological time. The dinosaurs existed in only one geological time, called the Mesozoic Era, which spanned from 252 to 66 million years ago.

COLOR THE TIMELINE

We divide time into "eras," which are then subdivided into "periods." Use the coloring key to color in each period (the smaller sections) on this timeline of life on Earth.

Eras:
- Precambrian
- Paleozoic Era
- Mesozoic Era
- Cenozoic Era

COLOR IT!

PRECAMBRIAN (4,600–542 MYA)

"The Age of Early Life" For billions of years, the only life on Earth was single-celled organisms in the seas. Later, multicellular animals evolved.

Herrerasaurus (heh-RARE-ra-SORE-us) was one of the earliest dinosaurs.

MESOZOIC ERA (252–66 MYA)

Triassic (252–201 mya)
The first dinosaurs and mammals appeared in this first of three periods known as "The Age of Dinosaurs."

Permian (299–252 mya)
The first reptiles as well as protomammals evolved and migrated across the planet during this period.

Carboniferous (358–299 mya)
This period saw an explosion of plants on land, including huge, tropical forests populated by giant insects.

A massive asteroid hit Earth.

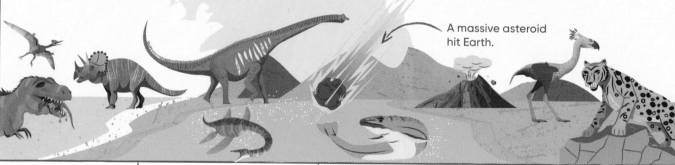

CENOZOIC ERA (66 MYA–PRESENT)

Jurassic (201–145 mya)
Many new types of dinosaurs emerged and spread out across the planet, becoming the dominant land animals.

Cretaceous (145–66 mya)
Dinosaurs thrived and grew bigger until 66 mya, when a catastrophic event wiped out all the dinosaurs except birds.

Paleogene (66–23 mya)
After the mass extinction of dinosaurs, life gradually recovered and the species left behind filled new niches.

Neogene (23–2 mya)
Forests were replaced by vast grasslands. Mammals evolved further, and huge sharks swam in the seas.

Coloring key
Periods:

Cambrian
Ordovician
Silurian
Devonian
Carboniferous
Permian
Triassic
Jurassic
Cretaceous
Paleogene
Neogene
Quaternary

PALEOZOIC ERA (542–252 MYA)

Cambrian (542–488 mya)
In this period, there was an explosion of life in the seas. The first fish with primitive backbones appeared.

Tiktaalik may have pulled itself up onto swampy banks.

Ordovician (488–444 mya)
Sea life diversified more in this period. There were strange jawless fish and creatures with external shells.

Cooksonia was one of the earliest land-living plants.

Devonian (416–358 mya)
This period was known as "The Age of Fishes," as fish with jaws swam in the seas and others climbed onto land.

Silurian (444–416 mya)
In the Silurian Period, plants began to colonize the land. Meanwhile, giant scorpions lived beneath the sea.

Our early ancestors appeared about 4 million years ago.

Quaternary (2 mya–present)
The Quaternary is our period in history. There were a series of ice ages, when mammoths roamed the grasslands.

MODERN **HUMANS** HAVE EXISTED FOR JUST **0.007%** OF EARTH'S HISTORY.

FIND THE CREATURES
Find the animals described below in the geological timeline on the left, then draw a picture of each of them.

DRAW IT!

a *Pterygotus (terry-GOAT-us)* was a huge sea scorpion that lived in the Silurian Period.

b *Lystrosaurus (LIS-trow-SORE-us)* was a protomammal with tusks from the Permian.

c *Sauroposeidon (SORE-oh-pos-i-den) was a colossal dinosaur from the Cretaceous.

NAME THAT ERA
Write the name of the era that the dinosaurs lived in. You can find the information on the left.

_ _ _ _ _ _ _ _ _ _ _ _ _

15

THE TRIASSIC PERIOD

The Triassic lasted from 252 to 201 million years ago (mya), and began just after a catastrophic mass extinction at the end of the Permian Period. Around 70 percent of life that had existed on Earth was now gone. The animals that survived quickly adapted to fill the empty space, and some entirely new types of animals appeared. This was the beginning of "The Age of Dinosaurs."

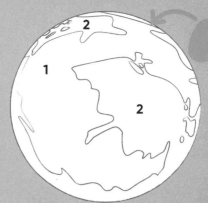

COLOR IT!

Key
1 Land
2 Sea

Triassic Earth
The Triassic world was hot, with little water except at the coasts and large expanses of desert. There was no grass or flowers and only a few types of plants. At the start of the period, there was just one huge supercontinent called Pangea.

DRAW THE ANIMALS
Dinosaurs weren't the only animals on Earth during the Triassic. Other types of animals had existed before the dinosaurs appeared and continued to live and evolve alongside them. Read the information in the panel on the right about each of the animals to help you work out where each of them goes in the scene. Then draw them in.

A lizardlike, land-living reptile

DRAW IT!

An early mammal

UNSCRAMBLE THE CREATURE
Cross out the letters in the word INSECT below, then rearrange the remaining letters to find the name of a Triassic creature that is still crawling around on Earth today.

A C I O H O E C
A R K T C N S C

_ _ _ _ _ _ _ _ _

WHO CAME FIRST?

The survivors of the Permian mass extinction included the animals that became dinosaurs. At first, dinosaurs were small, light carnivores that walked on two legs. Herbivores appeared later in the Triassic Period; some walked on two legs, others on four. Read about each of these Triassic dinosaurs, then number them in the order they appeared.

Coelophysis
(SEE-low-FYE-sis)
This theropod was a carnivore that hunted small creatures 220 mya, swallowing them whole. It walked on two legs and had slim, pointed jaws.

Herrerasaurus
(heh-RARE-ra-SORE-us)
This is one of the earliest known dinosaurs, from 231 mya. It was a carnivore and walked on two legs, using its tail for balance.

Plateosaurus
(PLATE-ee-oh-SORE-us)
This early, plant-eating relative of the sauropods lived 210 mya. It was about 26 feet (8 m) long and walked on its two back legs.

NUMBER IT!

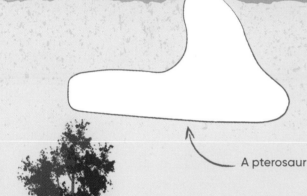

A pterosaur

A marine reptile

An insect

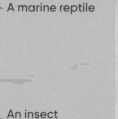

Eudimorphodon
(YOU-die-MOR-fo-don)
Flying reptiles appeared for the first time in the Triassic. This one was crow-sized.

Nothosaurus
(NO-tho-SORE-us)
Early marine reptiles, such as *Nothosaurus*, swam in Triassic seas at the same time as the first dinosaurs walked on land.

Megazostrodon
(MEG-ah-ZO-stroh-don)
The first mammals evolved in this period. This tiny, shrewlike one probably hunted insects.

Cockroach
Some insects survived the mass extinction. They bounced back more quickly than other animals, and a few are still around today.

Diphydontosaurus
(diff-eh-DONT-oh-SORE-us)
Land reptiles such as this lizardlike one thrived in the Triassic alongside dinosaurs.

THE JURASSIC PERIOD

The Jurassic was the middle period of the Mesozoic Era, from 201 to 145 million years ago (mya). Dinosaurs rapidly diversified, spreading across the planet and becoming the dominant land animals. Predatory groups of flesh-eating theropods grew larger, and long-necked sauropods became Earth's most successful herbivores. Ankylosaurs and stegosaurs also arrived on the scene.

COLOR IT!

Key
1 Land
2 Sea

Jurassic Earth
In the Jurassic Period, the climate was mild. Earth became wetter and cooler, allowing plant life to thrive. Pangea split into two giant continents: Laurasia in the north and Gondwana in the south.

HETERODONTOSAURUS
(HET-er-oh-DON-toe-SORE-us)

TYPE:	Ornithopod
WHEN:	....
HABITAT:	Shrublands
LENGTH:	3 feet (1 m)
DIET:	Plants, tubers, insects

CRYOLOPHOSAURUS
(cry-oh-LOAF-oh-SORE-us)

TYPE:	....
WHEN:	190–183 mya
HABITAT:	Forest and plains
LENGTH:	20 feet (6 m)
DIET:	Smaller dinosaurs

ARCHAEOPTERYX
(ar-kee-OP-ter-icks)

TYPE:	Theropod
WHEN:	151–146 mya
HABITAT:	Wooded Islands
LENGTH:	....
DIET:	Insects and small reptiles

SCELIDOSAURUS
(SKELL-ih-doe-SORE-us)

TYPE:	Ankylosaur
WHEN:	196–183 mya
HABITAT:	Forests
LENGTH:	13 feet (4 m)
DIET:	....

DIPLODOCUS
(dip-LOD-oh-kus)

TYPE:	Sauropod
WHEN:	154–150 mya
HABITAT:	....
LENGTH:	108 feet (33 m)
DIET:	Tree foliage

COMPLETE THE PROFILES
Dinosaurs of the Jurassic varied greatly. The first giant dinosaurs appeared in this period. Use the information below to complete the Jurassic dinosaur fact cards.

1.5 feet (45 cm)	Theropod
Plains with trees	
Plants	200–190 mya

FOLLOW THE PTEROSAURS

Pterosaurs became larger in the Jurassic. They swooped down from the skies to catch fish, clams, insects, and small mammals with their razor-sharp teeth. Follow these two pterosaurs to find out what they catch.

PTERODACTYLUS
(TEH-roe-DACK-till-us)

DEARC SGIATHANACH
(JARK ski-AN-och)

WHAT'S ITS NAME?

What was the middle geological period of the Mesozoic Era? Decode the letters below to find the answer.

T
E J
S H
I R
U C
A

WRITE IT!

_ _ _

_ _ _ _ _ _ _ _

DRAW IT!

THE EARLIEST **BIRDS,** OR AVIAN DINOSAURS, EVOLVED IN THE **JURASSIC.**

DRAW THE FOREST

Earth's first forests appeared during the Jurassic Period. They provided food for hungry herbivores, which were hunted in turn by fierce, predatory carnivores. Continue drawing this forest of trees for these sauropods to eat.

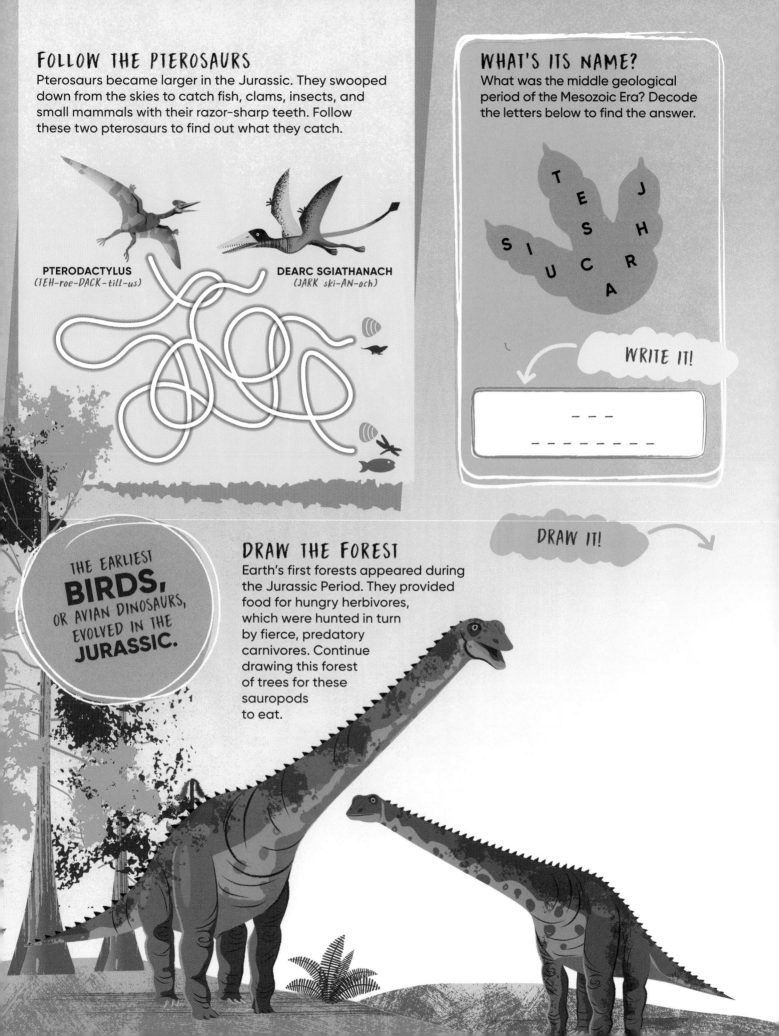

THE CRETACEOUS PERIOD

Dinosaurs diversified even further in the this period (145–66 million years ago). Some grew to immense sizes, becoming the biggest land animals Earth has ever seen. The Cretaceous ended abruptly—probably when Earth was hit by a large asteroid. Whatever happened, it caused a mass extinction, wiping out all the dinosaurs (except for birds).

COLOR IT!

Key
1 Land
2 Sea

Cretaceous Earth
Earth's climate remained wet and mild in the Cretaceous. The seasons became more varied, and flowering plants appeared for the first time. The continents Laurasia and Gondwana broke apart, and Earth's land masses began to move toward the positions they are in today.

Lythronax
(LIE-throw-nax)

Diabloceratops
(dee-AH-blow-SERRA-tops)

DRAW IT!

COMPLETE THE DINOSAUR SCENE
Tyrannosaurs were the top predators in the northern hemisphere of Cretaceous Earth. Here, the tyrannosaur *Lythronax* is looking for a meal. Follow the steps to complete the scene.

1. A *Diabloceratops* is in the middle of a battle, but its opponent is missing—draw it and color it in.

2. *Adelolophus* should be in a herd for safety—draw in some more of its family to keep this one company.

WHO AM I?

Read the descriptions of the Cretaceous dinosaurs below, then look at the statements on the card to work out whose picture you would see on the other side.

Alxasaurus
(ALK-sah-SORE-us)
Feathers covered the body of this two-legged dinosaur. Its teeth were blunt, which suggests it ate plants, not meat. Its huge stomach would have had space to digest large quantities of leaves.

WRITE IT!

I can walk on two legs.

I don't eat fish.

I don't have feathers.

I have a beak.

The crest on my nose is magnificent.

Who am I?

....

Hypsilophodon
(HIP-sih-LOAF-oh-don)
Small and swift, this herbivore would have been able to move quickly through the undergrowth to stay hidden from hungry predators. It had a narrow beak, big eyes, and a stiff tail, and it walked on two legs.

Baryonyx
(bah-ree-ON-iks)
This dinosaur lived in wetlands and walked on two legs. It had long, narrow jaws with lots of small teeth, strong arms, and sharp claws, which it probably used to catch fish.

Euoplocephalus
(YOU-owe-plo-SEFF-ah-lus)
This herbivore walked on four legs and was heavily armored. It had thick plates across its back, as well as a heavy club at the end of its tail for fighting off attackers.

Muttaburrasaurus
(MOO-tah-BUH-ruh-SORE-us)
This large herbivore could walk on either two legs or four. It had an inflatable crest on its nose and a sharp beak for slicing through tough vegetation.

Adelolophus
(ah-DEL-oh-LOW-fuss)

BONUS QUESTION
Which of the herbivores in this scene do you think looks like the easiest meal for *Lythronax*?

....

Mesozoic plant life

Here are some of the types of plants that would have lived alongside and been eaten by the dinosaurs. You might recognize them—similar plants are still found on Earth today.

Mosses
These small, simple plants were among the first to live on land rather than in water. They often grow in clumps in damp areas.

Ferns
Ferns have leaves called fronds. They don't have flowers, but reproduce using tiny, seedlike spores.

Conifers
These have small, pointed leaves called needles. They were the dominant plant of the Mesozoic and grew up to 100 feet (30 m) tall.

Horsetails
These plants have central stems with hairlike leaves. They have cones with spores at the top of the stems.

Flowering plants
These plants reproduce by using flowers with seeds. They first appeared in the early Cretaceous Period.

Cycads
Cycads have tough, fibrous leaves. Each plant is either male or female, and they reproduce using cones.

PREHISTORIC PLANTS

The plants that grew alongside the dinosaurs were not all the same as those we have on Earth today. The very earliest plants appeared long before the dinosaurs, but they were only able to live in water. Plants first moved onto land around 477 million years ago. Once there, they evolved and diversified into a range of different groups.

WHICH TYPE OF PLANT?

Paleontologists learn about ancient plants by studying their fossils. Use the Mesozoic plant life panel on the left to help you work out which group these three fossils belong to. Write the names under each fossil.

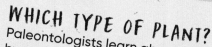

Flowering plant   Horsetail   Fern

WRITE IT!

Pecopteris

Magnolia

a ....

b ....

Equisetum

c ....

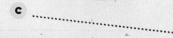

GUIDE THE BEETLE

By the end of the Cretaceous Period, there were flowering plants that were pollinated by insects. Draw a line that takes this beetle to every flower that doesn't have a beetle already sitting on it. Note: You can go up, down, and sideways, but you can't move diagonally or visit the same square twice.

FINISH HERE

GINKGO BILOBA
FRUITS SMELL DISGUSTING!
BUT SCIENTISTS THINK **DINOSAURS LOVED** THE SMELL!

DRAW IT!

DRAW THE GINKGO

Ginkgo trees have been around for 270 million years—dinosaurs would have eaten them. Use these steps to draw the last member of this ancient group, the *Ginkgo biloba* tree.

1. Look at the picture below and cover the tree branches with the distinct, fan-shaped leaves.
2. Draw some hanging nuts. (They turn orange in fall, when they are ripe and ready to eat.)
3. Add a long-necked dinosaur nibbling on them.

Ginkgo leaves and nuts

23

BODY BASICS

Fossils have taught us a lot about dinosaurs. We know what they ate, how they looked, and even some things about how they behaved. It has become evident that dinosaurs were very varied—and also that they had some things in common. Read on to find out about the basic body features that make a dinosaur a dinosaur.

T. REX **BABIES** WERE PROBABLY COVERED IN DUCKLINGLIKE **DOWNY** FEATHERS!

Common features

Here are the body features that scientists think were shared by all dinosaurs.

Bones
All dinosaurs were vertebrates—an animal with a backbone and a skeleton on the inside of its body. The skeleton was made from bone.

Teeth
With the odd exception, dinosaurs all had teeth—either razor sharp, for ripping meat, or wide and flat, for crushing tough plants.

Four limbs
All dinosaurs had four limbs. Some types walked on four sturdy legs, while others ran around on their two back legs.

Tails
All dinosaurs had tails. Some were longer than others, and some had particular uses, such as for balance or defense.

Skin
Dinosaurs had skin covering their bodies. Some had leathery scales, while others also developed a layer of feathers or bristles.

INVENT A DINOSAUR
Use the common features panel above to help you invent your own fantasy dinosaur. Its size, shape, and any special features are up to you—just make sure it includes all the body basics.

DRAW IT!

SCALES OR FEATHERS?

From fossil evidence, we know that dinosaurs had scales and many even had feathers or bristles, too. Some dinosaur fossils show the outline of full feathers. Others have bumps where the quills of feathers would once have attached. Draw lines to match each fossil to the correct dinosaur.

a

b

c

MATCH IT!

Edmontosaurus
(ed-MONT-oh-SORE-us)
This dinosaur's body was covered in interlinking circular scales.

Psittacosaurus
(si-tak-ah-SORE-us)
This dinosaur's tail had long, feathery quills along it.

Sinosauropteryx
(SIGH-no-sore-OP-ter-iks)
A fuzzy layer of simple feathers covered this dinosaur's body and tail.

FIND THE NEST

As far as we know, all dinosaurs laid eggs. Some even sat on their eggs to keep them warm, like many birds do today. Find the route through the tangle below to guide this *Citipati* (*SIH-tee-PAH-tee*) back to her empty nest.

START HERE

WHAT DID THEY EAT?

Most dinosaurs were plant-eaters (herbivores). Others were carnivores, who ate the herbivores, and smaller carnivores ... in fact, any other animals they could find. Not all dinosaurs stuck to either meat or plants. Some were omnivores and ate a wider range of foods.

Types of teeth
Like all animals, dinosaurs had teeth of different shapes, depending on what kind of food they ate.

Carnivores
Meat-eating dinosaurs had sharp, pointed teeth to slice through the flesh of mammals, fish, insects, and other dinosaurs.

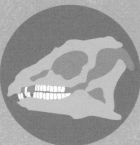

Omnivores
Dinosaurs that ate a variety of foods had a mixture of teeth—some for slicing and others for grinding.

Herbivores
Plant-eating dinosaurs had sharp beaks for stripping leaves off plants and wide, flat back teeth for grinding them up.

HERBIVORE OR CARNIVORE?
These dinosaurs are a mix of herbivores and carnivores. Look at their mouths and teeth, then check which of these you think they are.

Iguanodon
(ig-GWAH-no-don)
☐ Herbivore
☐ Carnivore

Spinosaurus
(SPINE-oh-SORE-us)
☐ Herbivore
☐ Carnivore

Styracosaurus
(sty-RACK-oh-SORE-us)
☐ Herbivore
☐ Carnivore

Carcharodontosaurus
(CAR-ka-roe-DON-toe-SORE-us)
☐ Herbivore
☐ Carnivore

Corythosaurus
(ko-RITH-oh-SORE-us)
☐ Herbivore
☐ Carnivore

CHECK IT!

WHAT'S FOR DINNER?

This is a food web from the Cretaceous Period. The arrows point from the living thing that gets eaten to the creature that eats it. Use the key below to color the arrows and complete the web. Can you circle the omnivores?

Arrow coloring key

➡ Animal prey

➡ Plant

TYRANNOSAURUS REX

ACHERORAPTOR

PACHYCEPHALOSAURUS

TREE FERN

TRICERATOPS

MAMMAL

ANKYLOSAURUS

INSECT

FLOWERS

COLOR IT!

FERN

CYCAD

CONIFER

SCIENTISTS LEARN ABOUT **DINOSAUR DIETS BY** STUDYING FOSSILIZED **DINOSAUR POOP.**

WHO EATS EVERYTHING?

What is the name for a dinosaur—or any animal—that eats both meat and plants? Unscramble these letters to spell the answer.

V

O   E   N   R   O

M

I

_ _ _ _ _ _ _ _

27

Dinosaur footprints

Different dinosaurs left behind different-shaped footprints. It's hard to tell exactly which dinosaur made a print. But experts can identify the type of dinosaur, because each type moved in a similar way. Here are some examples of this.

Theropods
These dinosaurs walked upright on two legs. They had three long, slender toes with pointed claws and V-shaped footprints.

Ornithopods
This group walked on two legs and left U-shaped prints. They had three rounded toes and spread their weight as they walked.

Sauropods
These were large, heavy dinosaurs that walked on four legs. Their tracks were deep, and their footprints are blob-shaped.

WALKING WITH DINOSAURS

How did dinosaurs walk? We can't watch them, but paleontologists are able to get an idea of dinosaur movement by studying the fossilized footprints dinosaurs left behind. Footprints are a type of trace fossil—fossils of an animal's activities rather than of its actual body parts.

THE WORLD'S **LONGEST** DINOSAUR **TRACKWAY** IS ON A CLIFF FACE **IN BOLIVIA,** SOUTH AMERICA.

COLOR IT!

COLOR THE PATHS
Color each type of footprint shown here in the same color to reveal the dino tracks. What kind of pathways can you see?

Coloring key

- Theropod
- Ornithopod
- Sauropod

REVEAL THE PRINTS

Which footprint is the **theropod**, which is the **ornithopod**, and which is the **sauropod**? First, join the dots. Then use the information on the left to decide which type of dinosaur made the print and label it.

DRAW IT!

a ....

b ....

c ....

WHO GOES THERE?

Dinosaur footprints show us how dinosaurs moved and if they walked alone or together in groups. Can you work out which type of dinosaur made each set of prints?

a Which type is traveling as a family?

☐ Sauropod
☐ Theropod
☐ Ornithopod

b Which type is chasing down its prey?

☐ Sauropod
☐ Theropod
☐ Ornithopod

c Which type is drinking at the stream?

☐ Sauropod
☐ Theropod
☐ Ornithopod

HUNTING

Carnivorous dinosaurs had to hunt or scavenge their meals. Big ones could eat lots of different kinds of food—from dead or sick dinosaurs to smaller dinosaurs they hunted. Smaller carnivores often ate lizards, mammals, and insects. Hunting could be dangerous, so carnivorous dinosaurs often avoided big prey—especially ones with spikes or other defenses.

CHECK IT!

WHO'S FOR DINNER?

This *Allosaurus* must decide which of these three dinosaurs would make the easiest prey to catch (without being injured). Read about its hunting tools and skills, then look at the stats on each card to decide.

STEGOSAURUS
(STEG-oh-SORE-us)

This slow-moving herbivore had bony plates along its back and a flexible tail with four sharp spikes.

LENGTH	WEIGHT
●●●●●●●○○○	●●●●●●○○○
FASTEST SPEED	**DEFENSE RATING**
●●●○○○○○○○	●●●●●●●●○○

ALLOSAURUS
(AL-oh-SORE-us)

This fast-running carnivore had sharp claws and bone-crunching jaws full of razor-sharp teeth.

LENGTH	WEIGHT
●●●●●●○○○○	●●●●○○○○○
FASTEST SPEED	**DEFENSE RATING**
●●●●○○○○○○	●●●●●○○○○○

COELURUS
(see-LURE-us)

This small carnivore had a mouth full of needlelike teeth for eating insects, lizards, and small mammals.

LENGTH	WEIGHT
●●○○○○○○○○	●●○○○○○○○○
FASTEST SPEED	**DEFENSE RATING**
●●●●●●●○○○	●●○○○○○○○○

APATOSAURUS
(a-PAT-oh-SORE-us)

This huge herbivore had four columnlike legs for trampling predators and a really long tail.

LENGTH	WEIGHT
●●●●○○○○○○	●●●●●●●●●●
FASTEST SPEED	**DEFENSE RATING**
●●○○○○○○○○	●●●●●●●●○○

GUIDE THE HUNTERS TO THEIR PREY

One exciting fossil find shows the remains of some meat-eating *Deinonychus* (*dye-NON-ee-cus*) around one *Tenontosaurus* (*ten-NON-toe-SORE-us*). It could mean they hunted as a team or were all attracted to the same kill and competed for it. Guide these four *Deinonychus* through the maze to the *Tenontosaurus*.

TENONTOSAURUS

DRAW IT!

NAME THE SCROUNGERS

Cross out the letters of the word CARNIVORE, then rearrange the remaining letters to spell the word for animals that eat other dead animals that they find.

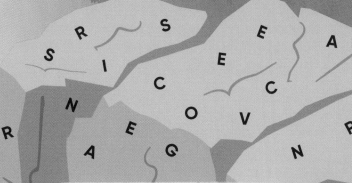

_ _ _ _ _ _ _ _ _

WRITE IT!

DINOSAUR DEFENSES

Herbivorous dinosaurs may have been hunted by the carnivorous dinosaurs, but they weren't totally helpless. Many of them had armor to protect their bodies and horns or clubbed tails that they could use to fight back.

IDENTIFY EACH DINOSAUR

Write letters beside each of the defensive descriptions below to match it to the correct dinosaur. You'll need to examine each dinosaur closely to make sure you don't get them mixed up.

Defensive body parts

Many plant-eating dinosaurs evolved body parts that helped them protect themselves. Here are a few examples.

Horns
Sharp horns on the head could be used to fight off attackers or compete with members of the same species.

Plate armor
Flat, bony plates called scutes protected dinosaur bodies from sharp teeth and razor-sharp claws.

Spikes
Spikes on the body made it harder for predators to get close and could be used to pierce an attacker's skin.

SOME **HERBIVORES ARE LIKELY TO HAVE LIVED IN HERDS** FOR PROTECTION.

WRITE IT!

 Barosaurus
(BAH-roe-SORE-us)
This dinosaur's enormous size made it hard for predators to attack, as they risked being trampled underfoot.

 Triceratops
(tri-SERRA-tops)
This dinosaur had a frill to protect its neck and three sharp horns: two on its forehead and one on its nose.

 Edmontonia
(ED-mon-TOE-nee-a)
Covered in thick body armor, this dinosaur also had spikes on its head, body, and tail.

 Styracosaurus
(sty-RACK-oh-SORE-us)
A neck frill adorned with long spikes, as well as a fearsome nose horn, protected this dinosaur.

 Stegosaurus
(STEG-oh-SORE-us)
With two rows of sharp plates along its back and spikes on its tail, this dinosaur was no easy meal.

 Iguanodon
(Ig-GWAH-no-don)
This dinosaur had sharp thumb spikes, which could puncture carnivores that came too close.

WHAT'S MY WEAPON?

Tails were really effective weapons. Herbivores used them to lash out and defend themselves. Some tails even had sharp spikes or heavy clubs at the end. Color in each dinosaur's outline to match the key below.

COLOR IT!

Colouring key

🦎 **Stegouros**
(STEG-oh-ROS)
This dinosaur's tail had rows of "blades" on each side, like an ancient Aztec warrior's weapon.

🦎 **Ankylosaurus**
(ANK-ill-oh-SORE-us)
This armored dinosaur had a huge, twin-sided tail club.

🦎 **Stegosaurus**
The tail on this dinosaur had four lethal spikes at the end.

e

f

CREATE A SUPER-DINO

Use this space to design defenses for your own imaginary dinosaur. Why not give it armored skin, lots of razor-sharp spikes, horns, and a scarily defensive tail?

DRAW IT!

WHICH IS WHICH?

Use the information on the right to help you work out what type of feather each is below. Beware, as one of them isn't a feather at all! Then finish the pictures.

COMPLETE IT!

a ....
....

b ....
....

c ....
....

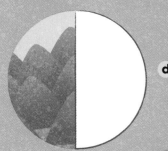

d ....
....

WRITE IT!

Bristle feather

Fluffy feather

Armored plates

Flight feather

FEATHERS

Recent fossil discoveries prove that some dinosaurs had feathers! This finding helped paleontologists make the evolutionary connection between dinosaurs and birds. Feathers would have been useful for staying warm and attracting potential mates. Eventually, the feathers became more complex, allowing some dinosaurs to fly.

Types of feathers

Dinosaur feathers changed and developed over time, from simple bristles into full feathers for flying.

Bristles
The earliest feathers were simple hollow tubes, poking up from scaly skin. Unlike modern feathers, they would have given dinosaurs a bristly texture, similar to coarse hair.

Fluff
Later, dinosaur feathers branched out. They developed thin filaments that spread out from a single point on the skin, creating a "fluffy" effect.

FEATHERS KEPT **PREDATORY DINOSAURS** WARM AT NIGHT WHILE **HUNTING** THEIR SLEEPING **PREY.**

Flight feathers
Eventually, dinosaurs developed fully formed flight feathers, similar to those of modern birds. Each feather had a central pole, with barbs sticking out from it on both sides.

COMPLETE THE WINGS

The first fossil discovered that showed evidence of feathers was of an *Archaeopteryx* (*ar-kee-OP-ter-icks*), which lived around 150 million years ago. Scientists believe it could fly through the air for short distances. Draw feathers to complete this drawing of *Archaeopteryx*.

This *Archaeopteryx* fossil clearly shows its feathered wings.

DRAW IT!

COLOR THE FEATHER

Not only do fossils reveal that dinosaurs had feathers, but also their colors. The dinosaur *Caihong juji* (*KIE-hong JU-ji*), for example, was as colorful as today's hummingbird. Use the key to color in this dinosaur neck feather.

Coloring key
1 2 3
4 5 6
7 8 9

COLOR IT!

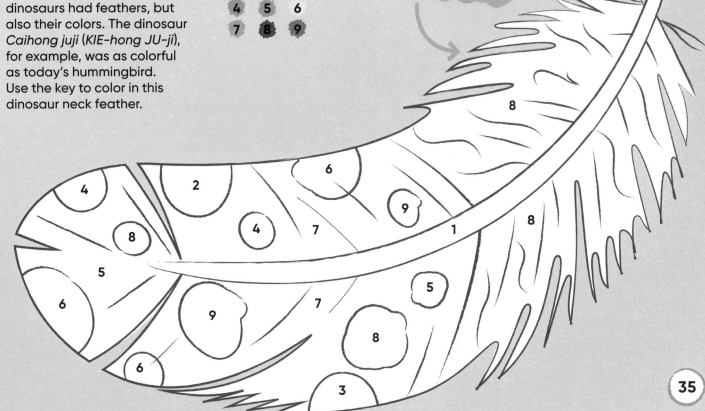

EGGS AND NESTS

We don't know much about how dinosaur families worked, but we do have some clues. The fossil record shows us that dinosaurs laid eggs, some made nests, and others may have cared for their eggs and protected them. Some species of dinosaurs even seem to have cared for their young.

Inside an egg

A few rare fossils of dinosaur eggs have the skeletons of unborn dinosaurs (embryos) preserved inside them. This helps scientists figure out which dinosaur laid the eggs and what baby dinosaurs might have looked like.

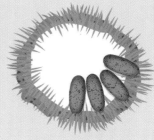

A stretchy membrane called the amniotic sac cushioned the embryo.

The embryo had large eyes.

The shell was usually hard like birds' eggs, but sometimes soft like turtle eggs.

The dinosaur embryo was curled up tight inside the egg.

While in the egg, the embryo was fed by the egg's yolk.

COLOR IT!

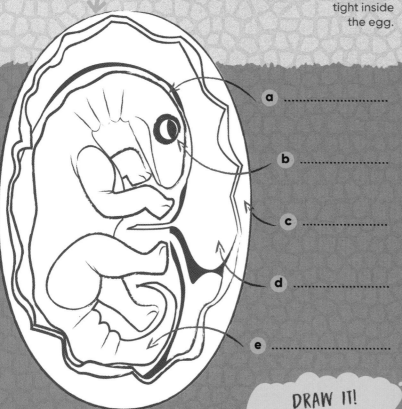

a ....

b ....

c ....

d ....

e ....

DRAW IT!

MATCH THE PARTS
Use the words in the box to complete the labels on this dinosaur egg. Then color it in.

Yolk	Embryo
Amniotic sac	
Eyes	Shell

FILL THE NESTS
Not all dinosaur nests were the same. Read about each of these nests and the eggs in them, then draw in some more eggs.

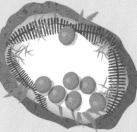

Oviraptor
(OVE-ee-rap-tor)
This dinosaur laid long eggs in a spiral pattern around the nest.

Maiasaura
(MY-a-SORE-ah)
These eggs were laid in an earth mound lined with plants.

Titanosaurus
(tie-TAN-oh-SORE-us)
This dinosaur laid large, almost spherical eggs.

WHICH ONE IS MY SHELL?

Dinosaur babies grew curled up tight inside an egg. Work out which of the babies on the right fits into each egg, then draw them inside it.

DRAW IT!

20 in (50 cm)

15 in (37 cm)

8 in (21 cm)

20 in (50 cm)
10 in (25 cm)
0 in (0 cm)

MAIASAURA

AEPYORNIS

GIGANTORAPTOR

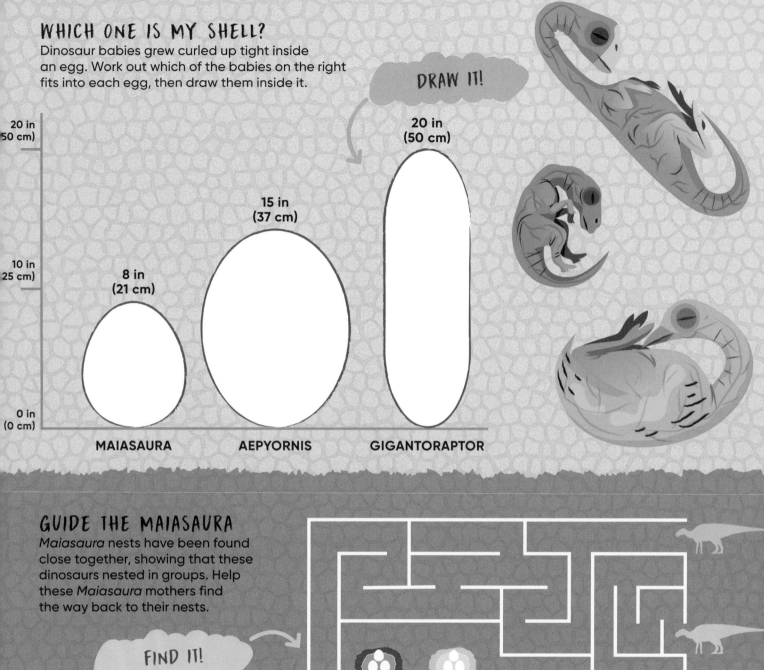

GUIDE THE MAIASAURA

Maiasaura nests have been found close together, showing that these dinosaurs nested in groups. Help these *Maiasaura* mothers find the way back to their nests.

FIND IT!

DINOSAUR GROUPS

More than 1,000 different dinosaur species have been named. They varied hugely in size, strength, speed, diet, and more. To help us understand all these dinosaurs, paleontologists have organized them into larger groups, based on shared features.

Theropods
Theropods walked on two legs, not four. The group includes many carnivores, such as *Tyrannosaurus rex* and *Velociraptor*.

Sauropods
Sauropods walked on four legs. They had long tails and long necks, and some of them reached enormous sizes.

COUNT THE DINOSAURS
One type of dinosaur outnumbers the others in this picture. Which dinosaur group is it? Compare the shapes and fill in the answer below.

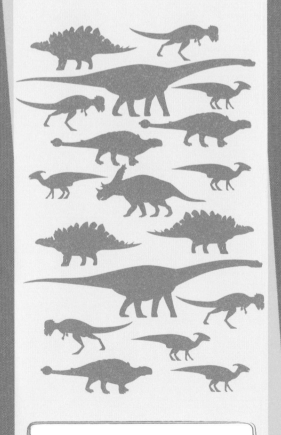

....

IDENTIFY THE HIPS
Work out which group these two dinos belong to from their hip bones.

1. Look at their hip bones and copy them in the spaces provided.

2. Then unscramble the letters and write the name of the dinosaur group.

DRAW IT!

SAUROPELTA

C H I N N I S O R T H I A

a In _ _ _ _ _ _ _ _ _ _ _ _ _ dinosaurs, both of the lower hip bones pointed backward.

ALLOSAURUS

N A S A R I C H U I S

b In _ _ _ _ _ _ _ _ _ _ _ dinosaurs, the lower hip bones pointed in opposite directions.

DINOSAURS

Ornithischians
These dinosaurs had "birdlike" hips, with hip bones that pointed backward.

Ankylosaurs
These four-legged dinos had thick body armor—like spikes on their backs and bony clubs on their tails.

Stegosaurs
Rows of bony plates or spikes ran along the backs of these four-legged herbivores.

Ornithopods
The ornithopods had birdlike feet and beaks. Some of them had elaborate crests on their heads.

Pachycephalosaurs
These dinos walked on two legs and probably used their thick, bony skulls against each other in battle.

Ceratopsians
Bony frills and sharp horns adorned the heavy skulls of these herbivores, which had a four-legged stance.

EODROMAEUS
(ee-oh-dro-MAY-us)
- [ ] Theropod
- [ ] Stegosaur

DIPLODOCUS
(dip-LOD-oh-kus)
- [ ] Pachycephalosaur
- [ ] Sauropod

SAUROPELTA
(SORE-oh-PELT-ah)
- [ ] Ankylosaur
- [ ] Ornithopod

CHECK IT!

WHICH GROUP?
Now test your knowledge about dinosaur groups. Check the box under each picture that shows the correct family for all these dinosaurs.

PARASAUROLOPHUS
(PA-ra-SORE-oh-LOAF-us)
- [ ] Ornithopod
- [ ] Sauropod

ACROTHOLUS
(ACK-roe-THO-luss)
- [ ] Ceratopsian
- [ ] Pachycephalosaur

SOME DINOSAURS WERE AS BIG AS **BLUE WHALES,** AND OTHERS AS TINY AS **PIGEONS.**

CHIALINGOSAURUS
(chi-ah-ling-oh-SORE-us)
- [ ] Stegosaur
- [ ] Theropod

PROTOCERATOPS
(PRO-toe-SERRA-tops)
- [ ] Ceratopsian
- [ ] Ankylosaur

THEROPODS

The theropods first appeared 230 million years ago, in the late Triassic Period. They were bipedal, which means they walked on two legs, not four. Most theropods were carnivores, although the group also includes some herbivores and omnivores. Theropods came in a huge range of sizes. Some were tiny and birdlike, while others were mighty apex predators.

Common features
The theropods were a huge and varied group of dinosaurs, but they all shared a few common features:

Back legs
They walked on their two back legs, which had three toes.

Front legs
Their front legs were small, with sharp, curved claws.

Mouth
They had mouths full of sharp, bladelike teeth for slicing flesh.

FILL IN THE FACTS
Use the word box to fill in the missing facts about these famous theropods.

20 feet (6 m)	Fish
Cretaceous	
USA	33 lb (15 kg)

TYRANNOSAURUS REX
(TIE-ran-oh-SORE-us REX)

WHEN:	Cretaceous
FOUND IN:	....
LENGTH:	39 feet (12 m)
WEIGHT:	9 tons (8 tonnes)
DIET:	Other animals

BARYONYX
(bah-ree-ON-iks)

WHEN:	Cretaceous
FOUND IN:	Europe
LENGTH:	23 feet (7 m)
WEIGHT:	1.2 tons (1 tonne)
DIET:	....

CAUDIPTERYX
(caw-DIP-ter-iks)

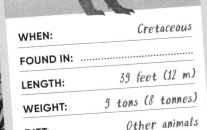

WHEN:	....
FOUND IN:	China
LENGTH:	3 feet (1 m)
WEIGHT:	5.5 lb (2.5 kg)
DIET:	Insects and plants

CERATOSAURUS
(Seh-RAT-oh-SORE-us)

WHEN:	Jurassic
FOUND IN:	USA, Portugal, and Tanzania
LENGTH:	....
WEIGHT:	1 ton (980 kg)
DIET:	Other animals

VELOCIRAPTOR
(vel-OSS-ee-RAP-tor)

WHEN:	Cretaceous
FOUND IN:	Mongolia and China
LENGTH:	6.5 feet (2 m)
WEIGHT:	....
DIET:	Other animals

CAMOUFLAGE OR DISPLAY?

Only a few dinosaur fossils contain evidence of color. To draw dinosaurs, we have to make assumptions about what color they may be. Try coloring in these theropods in two different ways to match the descriptions below.

WRITE IT!

COLOR IT!

SCIENTISTS NOW BELIEVE THAT **MOST THEROPODS,** INCLUDING T. REX, HAD **FEATHERS** OR BRISTLES!

FIND THE LIVING THEROPODS

One group of theropods is still alive today. Unscramble the letters below to reveal which of the animals around you are living dinosaurs.

D I S B R

_ _ _ _ _

Display
Some scientists have suggested that dinosaurs would have had bright colors, similar to some modern birds.

Camouflage
Dinosaurs are often shown in green and brown colors, which would have provided them with camouflage.

41

COMPLETE THE KILLING TEETH

T. rex's jaws contained around 60 razor-sharp, backward-facing teeth, some as big as 8 in (20 cm) long. Use the picture on the right to help you draw the missing teeth on this *T. rex* skull.

DRAW IT!

Big eyeballs
These were the size of an adult human's clenched fist.

WHY SUCH TINY ARMS?

Paleontologists are mystified by *T. rex*'s tiny arms. They weren't long enough to reach its mouth or catch prey—despite having 4 in (10 cm) claws on each finger. Which theory below do you think explains their size? Hint: There is no right or wrong answer.

- ☐ Helping *T. rex* get up after resting
- ☐ Holding onto wriggling prey
- ☐ Avoiding losing an arm in a fight
- ☐ Or write your own theory here:
....
....

Muscular back legs
These had to be strong to support up to 9 tons (8 tonnes) of dinosaur above.

SPOTLIGHT ON:
TYRANNOSAURUS REX

The most famous dinosaur of all time is *Tyrannosaurus rex*, known as *T. rex* for short. This theropod was a fearsome apex predator that swallowed small dinosaurs whole. In its own habitat, *T. rex* was at the top of the Cretaceous food chain—its name means "king of the tyrant lizards."

Huge toes
Like all theropods, *T. rex* had three toes on each foot.

TYRANNOSAURUS REX

When: 68–66 million years ago (mya)
Habitat: Forest and swamps
Length: 39 feet (12 m)
Diet: Other dinosaurs
Pronunciation: TIE-ran-oh-SORE-us REX

Thick tail
T. rex would have used its long tail to help balance the weight of its huge head at the front.

THE WORLD'S **LARGEST** AND MOST COMPLETE **T. REX SKELETON** IS IN CHICAGO'S FIELD MUSEUM AND IS NAMED **SUE.**

DRAW IT!

16.4 FEET (5 M)

13 FEET (4 M)

9.8 FEET (3 M)

6.6 FEET (2 M)

3.3 FEET (1 M)

0 FEET (0 M)

DRAW THE MIGHTY PREDATOR

At around 13 feet (4 m) tall, *T. rex* was more than twice the height of an average human adult. Use the scale to draw one beside this person. Luckily for us, *T. rex* lived long before we appeared on Earth!

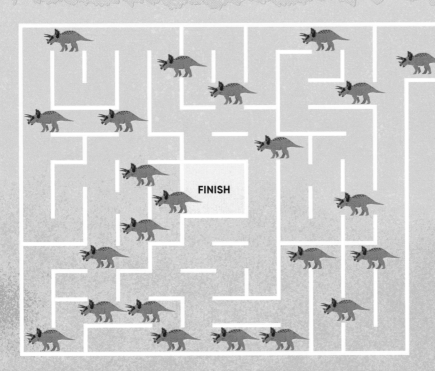

FINISH

START HERE

HUNT THE DINOS

T. rex ate other dinosaurs. Its tooth marks have been found on many dinosaur bones, including those of *Triceratops*. Guide this *T. rex* through the maze so that it captures all the *Triceratops* without crossing its own path.

SPOTLIGHT ON:
SPINOSAURUS

No dinosaurs lived in water, but *Spinosaurus* came close. It lived on swampy flood plains and probably spent a lot of time in and around the rivers and lakes, hunting for supersized fish. *Spinosaurus* had a tall sail of bones covered by skin extending up from its back, which seems to be unique among the dinosaurs. It also had a long snout full of sharp teeth for fishing.

SPINOSAURUS WAS **FOUR** TIMES **HEAVIER** THAN AN **ELEPHANT.**

The "sail" was 6.5 feet (2 m) high and made of long struts sticking out from its spine, covered in skin.

The skin is likely to have been covered in scales.

SPINOSAURUS

When: 100-93 mya (Late Cretaceous)
Habitat: Tropical swamps
Length: 52 feet (16 m)
Diet: Fish
Pronunciation: SPINE-oh-SORE-us

The powerful arms and hands had long, curved claws for holding onto slippery fish.

Some scientists believe *Spinosaurus* may have had webbed toes for swimming.

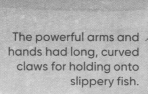

Onchopristis
This giant sawfish could grow to 16 feet (5 m) in length and swam in the waters where *Spinosaurus* hunted.

Mawsonia
This fish had lots of fins and a lobed tail and was probably on *Spinosaurus*'s menu. Its relatives still exist today and haven't changed very much in 390 million years.

CATCH THE FISH

It is likely that *Spinosaurus* hunted large fish in the Late Cretaceous waters of what is now North Africa. Draw a line to connect each *Spinosaurus* with a fish of the same color. You can move up, down, and across (but not diagonally), and the lines must not cross.

MATCH IT!

Its long jaws were similar to those of a modern crocodile, with longer teeth at the front for catching fish.

COLOR THE GIANT HUNTER

Spinosaurus is the largest carnivorous dinosaur ever discovered—growing up to 52 feet (16 m) in length. Paleontologists are unsure what the tall "sail" on its back was for, but they think it could have been brightly colored for display. Decide for yourself when you color in this *Spinosaurus*.

COLOR IT!

SPOTLIGHT ON:
VELOCIRAPTOR

This dinosaur was a fierce predator, despite being no bigger than a large turkey. It probably ambushed its prey like a modern eagle does—pinning it down with long claws and tearing it apart with its 56 razor-sharp teeth. We know that *Velociraptor* had feathers, but it couldn't fly—they were probably for keeping warm on cold desert nights.

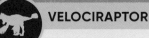

VELOCIRAPTOR

When: 74-70 mya (Late Cretaceous)
Habitat: Deserts
Length: 6 feet (1.8 m)
Diet: Other animals
Pronunciation: vel-OSS-ee-RAP-tor

Keen eyesight
Velociraptor had large eyes and good nighttime vision, which was important for hunting its prey.

Feathery tail
Its long, bony tail may have had a fringe of feathers.

Deadly hunter

Velociraptor was an agile hunter, pouncing on its prey at lightning speed. Dinosaurs (such as *Protoceratops*) and small mammals were its likely prey, which it would have stalked at night or twilight near scarce watering holes.

Sickle-shaped back claw
The claw on the second toe grew to 2.5 in (6.5 cm) long.

HUNT WITH VELOCIRAPTOR

Fossilized eye bones of *Velociraptor* suggest that it was a nocturnal hunter, ambushing its prey at twilight or nighttime. As a small dinosaur, it had to choose its prey carefully. Read about a day in its life and draw a picture for each stage.

VELOCIRAPTOR LIVED IN WHAT IS NOW **MONGOLIA** AND **CHINA.**

DRAW IT!

It is daytime, and the *Velociraptor* is curled up under a low tree branch, soundly asleep.

As dusk falls, she wakes up hungry and thirsty and heads for a watering hole. She spies a *Protoceratops*.

2 p.m.

7 p.m.

SEE THROUGH THEIR EYES

Velociraptor had good night vision. So did Cretaceous mammals, such as *Zalambdalestes*. But dinosaurs like *Protoceratops* were equipped for life in daylight. Use the coloring key to reveal the difference between what each potential prey saw at night.

Coloring key

COLOR IT!

What *Protoceratops* saw
Diurnal (daytime) animals have smaller pupils and receptors for seeing things clearly during the day but not at night.

What *Zalambdalestes* saw
Nocturnal (nighttime) animals have wider pupils to allow more light in and special receptors at the back of the eyes to help them see in low light.

Protoceratops
(PRO-toe-SERRA-tops)
This ceratopsian had small horns, but its beaky mouth could give a powerful bite.

Zalambdalestes
(ZAH-lam-da-LESS-tease)
New types of mammals had appeared in the Cretaceous deserts of Mongolia, such as this shrewlike one.

SPOT THE IMPOSTOR!

Each of *Velociraptor*'s feet had an extra-long, curved talon. It was held up off the ground, away from the other claws, and would have been used for subduing wriggling prey. Circle the dinosaur here that's not a *Velociraptor*.

As she prepares to ambush her prey, she catches the scent of an easier meal— a small mammal.

The mammal darts away as *Velociraptor* pounces, because it also has good nighttime vision.

Velociraptor spots a dead *Protoceratops* in the distance, which is a safer meal than the live one.

The Sun is beginning to rise, and *Velociraptor* prepares to sleep again after her feast.

7:30 p.m.   7:45 p.m.   9 p.m.   5 a.m.

SAUROPODS

The sauropods had long necks and wide legs and were colossal in size. They were herbivores that ate constantly to keep their enormous bodies moving. Their long necks allowed them to reach leaves high up in the trees, in a similar way to modern giraffes.

Sauropod family

The dinosaurs in this group were all large, with long necks and tails. Some were gigantic, like *Giraffatitan*, while others were lighter with smaller bodies, such as *Omeisaurus* (oh-may-SORE-us). Here are some of this amazing dinosaur family, which lived all across the world during the Jurassic and Cretaceous Periods.

This sauropod could reach higher into the trees to feed due to its longer front legs.

This Cretaceous sauropod had bony armor plating with spikes on its back for protection.

ALAMOSAURUS

BRACHIOSAURUS

SALTASAURUS

OMEISAURUS

WHO AM I?

Can you help create a passport for this huge sauropod by filling in the spaces below with all the correct information? Don't forget to draw its passport photo, too.

NAME:

COUNTRY:

LENGTH:

I LIKE TO EAT:

SIGNED:

WRITE IT!

This sauropod had a relatively small head but a huge body.

SAUROPOSEIDON

APATOSAURUS

MAMENCHISAURUS

This sauropod had the longest neck—up to 43 feet (13 m) long.

DIPLODOCUS

GIRAFFATITAN

When: 155–145 mya (Late Jurassic)

Habitat: Open plains and forests in what is now Tanzania, Africa

Length: 85 feet (26 m)

Diet: Tree leaves

Pronunciation:
ji-RAF-a-TIE-tan

TRUE OR FALSE?

It takes a lot of energy to grow the extra bone and muscle in a long neck. So what do you think sauropods gained from having such long necks?

a It allowed them to eat food that smaller herbivores couldn't reach.

☐ True ☐ False

b Long necks helped them stay warm in wintertime.

☐ True ☐ False

c With their heads up so high, they could see danger coming from far off.

☐ True ☐ False

d They could run faster by using their neck as an extra leg.

☐ True ☐ False

FIND THE EGGS

A sauropod has laid its eggs below. Each egg weighs about 11 lb (5 kg), twice the size of an ostrich egg. How many eggs can you find hidden in the undergrowth?

WRITE IT!

49

Too large to eat

These giants roamed across the semiarid plains of what is now Argentina, South America, nibbling on high treetops. They grew too big to be easily preyed upon by carnivores.

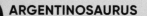

ARGENTINOSAURUS

When: 96-94 mya (Late Cretaceous)
Habitat: Forests and plains
Length: 115 feet (35 m)
Diet: Plants
Pronunciation: AR-jen-TEEN-oh-SORE-us

SPOTLIGHT ON: ARGENTINOSAURUS

The titanosaurs were a group of supersized sauropods with long necks; long tails; and four sturdy, pillarlike legs. Some of them grew to incredible dimensions, and *Argentinosaurus* is likely to have been one of the biggest of all. It's hard to know for certain because only a handful of its bones have ever been found.

DRAW A TITANO-HUMAN

Argentinosaurus babies were 3.3 feet (1 m) long when they hatched but grew to 35 times that size as adults! A human baby is about 19 in (50 cm) long at birth. Imagine if we grew to 35 times that size as adults! Use the grid to draw a "Titano-human" adult here.

DRAW IT!

FOSSILIZED **NESTS SHOW** ARGENTINOSAURUS **LAID ABOUT** **15** SOCCER BALL-SIZED **EGGS.**

HUMAN BABY

TITANO-HUMAN

The babies were tiny next to the adults. They were vulnerable, so had to grow very fast.

BALANCE THE SCALES

Argentinosaurus may have been the biggest dinosaur of all time—it's a contest between it and *Patagotitan* (*pat-AG-oh-tie-tan*). Can you work out how many male African elephants it would take to balance out one *Argentinosaurus*, then draw them on the scale?

DRAW IT!

This adult *Argentinosaurus* = 96 tons (88 tonnes)
A male African elephant = 6 tons (5.5 tonnes)

FIND IT!

SEARCH THE SKIN

Argentinosaurus's skin would have been covered in a layer of thick scales. Find the word for the group of giant sauropods that *Argentinosaurus* belonged to in this scaly grid and write it below.

_ _ _ _ _ _ _ _ _ _ _ _ _

STEGOSAURS

This group of spiky dinosaurs were slow-moving herbivores that walked on four legs. They first appeared in the middle of the Jurassic Period and died out early in the Cretaceous. Their most distinctive feature was the rows of bony plates that ran along their backs. Some species also had spikes on their shoulders and tails.

How to spot a stegosaur
These are the features to look out for on a stegosaur:

Defensive spikes
A double row of plates or spikes along the middle of the dinosaur's back.

Narrow head
A long, narrow head with eyes on either side helped stegosaurs keep a lookout for predators.

Beaklike mouth
A beak-shaped mouth allowed these herbivores to grip and tear the plants they ate.

Walks on four legs
Stegosaurs walked on two pairs of legs, with shorter front legs and longer back legs.

KENTROSAURUS **MAY HAVE SWUNG ITS TAIL AT SPEEDS OF 22 MPH** (36 KPH).

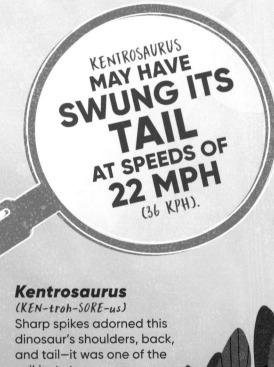

Kentrosaurus
(KEN-troh-SORE-us)
Sharp spikes adorned this dinosaur's shoulders, back, and tail—it was one of the spikiest stegosaurs.

DRAW IT!

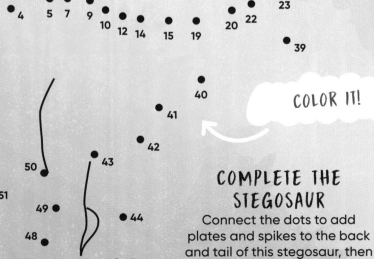

COLOR IT!

COMPLETE THE STEGOSAUR
Connect the dots to add plates and spikes to the back and tail of this stegosaur, then color it in to finish the picture.

52

FILL IN THE FACTS

Stegosaurs evolved from two-legged dinosaurs that looked quite different to them, such as the tiny *Scutellosaurus*. This proto-stegosaur had rows of smaller armored plates than its later relatives. Use the information below to fill in the card about *Scutellosaurus* on the right.

> 3 feet (1 m) Early Jurassic
>
> USA *Scutellosaurus*

NAME:
....
SAID:
SKOO-tell-oh-SORE-us
WHERE:
....
WHEN:
....
HABITAT:
Floodplains
LENGTH:
....
DIET:
Herbivore

WRITE IT!

FIND THE IMPOSTORS

Two of these dinosaurs are not stegosaurs. Use the information in the "How to spot a stegosaur" box to work out which are the impostors, then check one box under each dinosaur.

TRICERATOPS

☐ Stegosaur   ☐ Not a stegosaur

HUAYANGOSAURUS

☐ Stegosaur   ☐ Not a stegosaur

ANKYLOSAURUS

☐ Stegosaur   ☐ Not a stegosaur

LEXOVISAURUS

☐ Stegosaur   ☐ Not a stegosaur

MIRAGAIA

CHECK IT!

☐ Stegosaur   ☐ Not a stegosaur

SPOTLIGHT ON:
STEGOSAURUS

Stegosaurus had an impressive array of bony plates running down its back and sharp spikes at the end of its tail. However, this was not an aggressive dinosaur—it was a herbivore, and it spent its days eating all the plants it could find.

FIND THE FOOD

Stegosaurus ate low-growing plants. Read the descriptions beside each circle and find the plant on these pages. Then draw it.

Cycads
These plants usually have a crown of leaves, with all the leaves growing out from a central point. They don't have flowers.

Ferns
These plants have delicate fronds branching out from a central stem. The leaves start off tightly curled, then unfurl as they grow.

Horsetails
These plants grow in sandy or gravelly soil. Instead of flowers, they have cones with spores at the top of their thin stems.

DRAW IT!

COLOR THE PLATES

The plates on a *Stegosaurus*'s back were made of bone. They may have been used to help the dinosaur control its body temperature. They might also have been used for display—to attract a mate. Color in the plates of this *Stegosaurus*, so they are eye-catching and bright, to stand out.

Stegosaurus had a small head and a brain the size of a dog's, which was tiny for a dinosaur of its size.

COLOR IT!

Sharp beak for slicing through plants

The throat was protected by thick, flexible scales.

STEGOSAURUS

When: 155–151 mya (Late Jurassic)
Habitat: Forests
Length: 30 feet (9 m)
Diet: Leaves and ferns
Pronunciation: STEG-oh-SORE-us

AVOID THE ALLOSAURUS!

Stegosaurus was often hunted by the theropod *Allosaurus*. Follow the instructions to find a safe route for this one through the grid to eat the cycad plant:

1. Add three more *Allosaurus* in squares (A,4), (B,2), and (C,1).

2. Now draw a safe route through the grid for the *Stegosaurus* to take to avoid them all. Note: It shouldn't cross its own path and can't move diagonally.

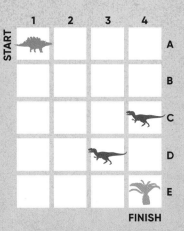

USE YOUR BRAINPOWER

Stegosaurus had a tiny brain for its size—eating plants didn't require much brainpower. Which of these skulls belongs to a *Stegosaurus*? Unscramble the letters to find which four animals these skulls belong to, then write it underneath.

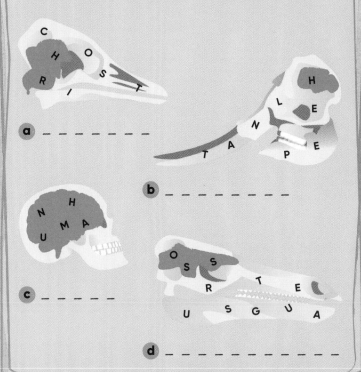

a _ _ _ _ _ _ _ _

b _ _ _ _ _ _ _

c _ _ _ _ _

d _ _ _ _ _ _ _ _ _ _

The hind legs were longer than the front legs. *Stegosaurus* may have been able to stand on its hind legs for short periods of time.

Spikes on the tail would have been used for defense against predators.

ANKYLOSAURS

With bodies close to the ground and heavy armor, this group of dinosaurs were built like tanks. They evolved armor for defense—with thick skulls and fused, bony plates on their necks and backs, often studded with spikes. Any predator wanting to eat an ankylosaur would have had to get past all that armor and weaponry.

WHICH ANKYLOSAUR IS WHICH?

These descriptions of ankylosaurs have been separated from their images. Write the letter next to the correct description.

Common features

Some ankylosaurs had clubs on their tails or horns on their heads, but all of them shared some features:

Four legs
Ankylosaurs were heavy, so they walked on four stumpy legs.

Bony plates
Armored, bony plates provided protection from predators' claws.

Horny beak
Ankylosaurs used their horny beaks to strip leaves from plants.

MATCH IT!

Sauropelta (SORE-oh-PELT-ah)
.... Large spines extended from this ankylosaur's neck and shoulders. Its back was covered in a thick layer of bony plates.

Gastonia (gas-TOE-nee-ah)
.... This ankylosaur had rows of sharp spines along its body, as well as long spikes all down each side of its body and tail.

Gargoyleosaurus (GAR-goil-oh-SORE-us)
.... This was one of the earliest ankylosaurs and was smaller than most of the others. It had horns on its head and cheeks and spines on its head and back.

Ankylosaurus (ANK-ill-oh-SORE-us)
.... This was the biggest ankylosaur. It had a huge tail club made of solid bone and bony plates across its whole body, as well as four horns on its face.

ADD THE ARMOR

This ankylosaur has no protective armor! Follow the steps below to complete its bony defenses.

1. First, the tail. You could add spikes running along it, a heavy club at the end, or even both.

2. Some ankylosaurs had spikes sticking out around their necks and along their shoulders, too.

3. Finally, add heavy, bony plates to your ankylosaur's body. Your plates could include studs or spikes.

DRAW IT!

ANKYLOSAURS **WERE THE BEST PROTECTED** OF ALL DINOSAURS.

WHAT TO EAT?

Ankylosaurs were herbivores. They used their horny beaks to slice through plants and to gather seeds and small fruits. Here are a number of foods—check those that would have appealed to an ankylosaur.

FERN
☐ Eat

FISH
☐ Eat

MEAT
☐ Eat

SEEDS
☐ Eat

UNSCRAMBLE THE NAMES

The names of these ankylosaurs have been mixed up. Unscramble the letters and write the names into the spaces below.

R O S A P E U L T A

a _ _ _ _ _ _ _ _ _ _

L E O S A G O Y U R A R G U S

b _ _ _ _ _ _ _ _ _ _ _ _ _

FILL IN THE FACTS

Use the word box below to complete these fact cards of famous ornithopods.

30 feet (9 m)

4.4 tons (4 tonnes)

Early Cretaceous

6 feet (2 m)

(MY-a-SORE-ah)

IGUANODON
(ig-GWAH-no-don)

This large ornithopod had long arms and could move on four legs as well as two. It had bony spikes on its thumbs for defense.

WHEN:	Early Cretaceous
LENGTH:	....
WEIGHT:	4.4 tons (4 tonnes)

IGUANODON WAS THE FIRST **PLANT-EATING DINOSAUR** TO BE CLASSIFIED AS **A DINOSAUR.**

OURANOSAURUS
(oo-RAN-oh-SORE-us)

This ornithopod had a row of spines sticking up from its backbone that gave it a high, hump-backed appearance.

WHEN:	....
LENGTH:	23 feet (7 m)
WEIGHT:	2.4 tons (2.2 tonnes)

HYPSILOPHODON
(HIP-sih-LOAF-oh-don)

This dinosaur was able to run fast to escape predators. It had a long tail to help it balance and sharp teeth for slicing through plants.

WHEN:	Early Cretaceous
LENGTH:	....
WEIGHT:	130 lb (60 kg)

MAIASAURA

This ornithopod lived in herds where hundreds of adults took care of their babies together.

WHEN:	....
LENGTH:	Late Cretaceous
WEIGHT:	30 feet (9 m)
	....

ORNITHOPODS

The ornithopods were one of the most successful groups of dinosaurs—they survived over a long period of time and evolved into many different species. The first ornithopods were small and walked on two legs. Many later species were bigger, walked on four legs, and had teeth that were adapted to grind up their food.

Common features

Although there were many different types of ornithopods, they all shared a few common features:

Plant-eaters
They were all herbivores. Some stood on two legs to reach high branches.

Short beaks
They all had short, horned beaks for cropping vegetation.

Bipedal gait
Most walked on two legs, but some walked on four legs or could do both.

CONNECT THE HERD

Ornithopods had no armor, so some lived in herds for safety. Draw lines to connect the members of this herd of *Shantungosaurus* (*shan-TUN-go-SORE-us*). The numbers in the circles on their backs tell you how many lines each animal should have connected to it.

COMPLETE THE CRESTS

The hadrosaurs (duck-billed dinosaurs) were ornithopods with beaks a bit like those of modern ducks. Some of them also had crests on their heads for display. Color the crest of the second hadrosaur, then draw your own on the third one. Be creative, as we can't be sure what colors or patterns were on their crests.

DRAW IT!

CORYTHOSAURUS
(*ko-RITH-oh-SORE-us*)

OLOROTITAN
(*oh-LOR-oh-TIE-tan*)

FIND THE GROUP

This word has been jumbled up by a *Parasaurolophus* call! Can you unscramble the letters to find a word for the subgroup these dinosaurs belonged to?

O U S
R A
D
A
S H R

_ _ _ _ _ _ _ _ _ _

WRITE IT!

Hard beak
A ducklike beak was used for slicing through tough plants.

Crest
Parasaurolophus's long, bony crest was part of its skull.

HOW DID PARASAUROLOPHUS CALL?

We don't know what dinosaurs sounded like, but the skull of *Parasaurolophus* gives us some clues. Scientists believe it took a deep breath, closed its mouth, and blew air out of its nostrils to make low, trumpeting calls. Draw arrows inside this crest to show the direction the air flowed.

DRAW IT!

Powerful arms
Strong arms allowed *Parasaurolophus* to walk on four legs, as well as two.

SPOTLIGHT ON:
PARASAUROLOPHUS

Parasaurolophus belonged to a subgroup of the ornithopods called hadrosaurs. They were also known as duck-billed dinosaurs because of their broad, flattened snouts and toothless beaks. A sweeping crest made this dino stand out from the crowd, and allowed *Parasaurolophus* to make itself heard.

 PARASAUROLOPHUS

When: 83-71 mya (Late Cretaceous)
Habitat: Dense forests
Length: 31 feet (9.5 m)
Diet: Leaves
Pronunciation:
PA-ra-SORE-oh-LOAF-us

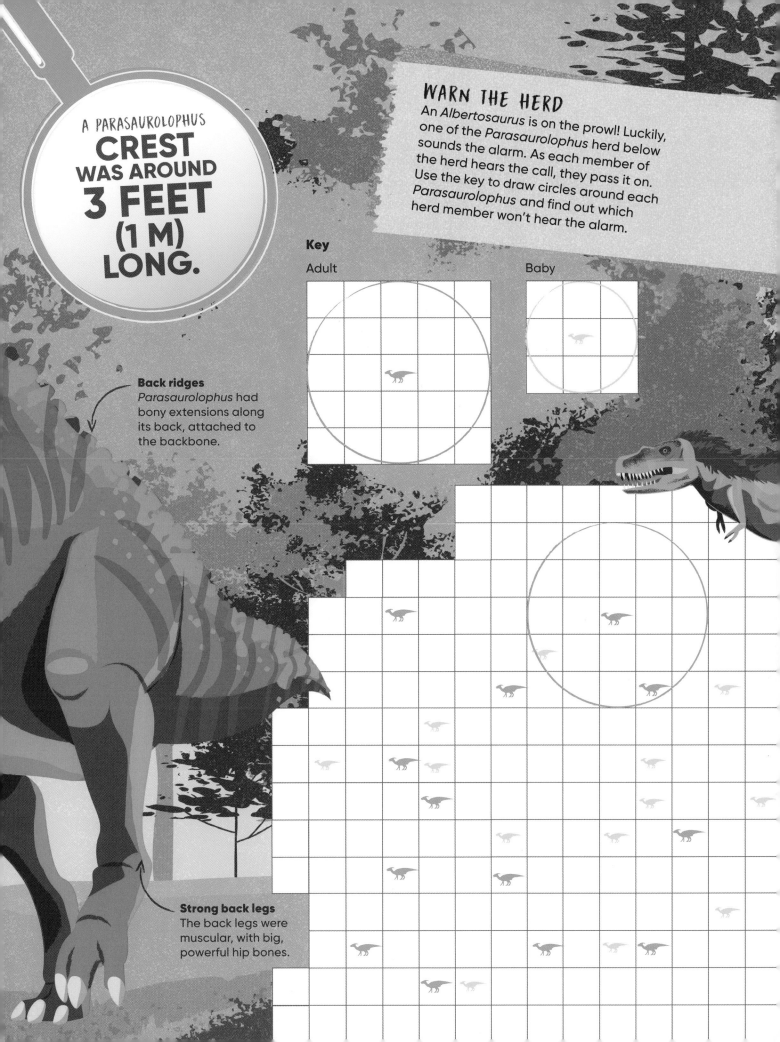

A PARASAUROLOPHUS **CREST WAS AROUND 3 FEET (1 M) LONG.**

Back ridges
Parasaurolophus had bony extensions along its back, attached to the backbone.

Strong back legs
The back legs were muscular, with big, powerful hip bones.

WARN THE HERD
An *Albertosaurus* is on the prowl! Luckily, one of the *Parasaurolophus* herd below sounds the alarm. As each member of the herd hears the call, they pass it on. Use the key to draw circles around each *Parasaurolophus* and find out which herd member won't hear the alarm.

Key

Adult

Baby

PACHYCEPHALOSAURS

At the end of the Mesozoic, a new group of dinosaurs appeared—the pachycephalosaurs. Fossils for this group of dinosaurs are rare, and no complete skeletons have been found so far, which makes the group quite mysterious. However, we do know that the pachycephalosaurs walked on two legs, were herbivores or possibly omnivores, and had thick domes of bone on top of their skulls.

Pachycephalosaurus

The most famous of the bone-headed dinosaurs is *Pachycephalosaurus*, which translates to "thick-headed lizard." Paleontologists think its domed head may have been used for fighting or to display to other dinosaurs.

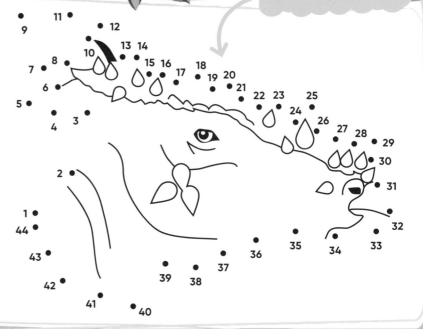

The skull featured a number of bony spikes and bumps.

The short, beaked mouth was similar to that of a bird.

Four toes on each foot

PACHYCEPHALOSAURUS

When: 71-66 mya (Late Cretaceous)
Habitat: Forests
Length: 14.5 feet (4.5 m)
Diet: Plants, nuts, and fruit
Pronunciation:
PACK-ee-SEF-ah-low-SORE-us

DRAW IT!

REVEAL THE YOUNG ONE

Some fossilized skulls have been found with more elaborate bumps and horns and a flat head instead of the dome. Scientists now think these skulls may have belonged to young *Pachycephalosaurus*. Connect the dots to find out what they looked like.

SOME
PACHYCEPHALOSAUR
SKULLS
WERE
9 INCHES
(23 CM)
THICK!

COLOR ME IN!

Color in this second *Pachycephalosaurus*. It doesn't need to be the same as the one on the left, because it might be from a different herd.

COLOR IT!

The body was probably covered in thick, scaly skin.

Long, thick tail, for balance

Strong back legs supported the dinosaur's weight.

CLASH THE HEADS

It has been suggested that male pachycephalosaurs clashed their hefty skulls together in head-butting battles, just like modern rams. Track each pachycephalosaur's journey on the grid using the instructions below and put a cross in the square where they meet to clash heads.

1. Move 3 squares right and 5 squares up

2. Move 1 square down and 2 squares left

3. Move 3 squares left

4. Move 5 squares down and 2 squares left

5. Move 2 squares up and 5 squares right

6. Move 6 squares up

	A	B	C	D	E	F	G	H	I	J
8										START
7										
6										
5										
4										
3										
2										
1										

START

WHAT'S THEIR OTHER NAME?

Find the letters in *Pachycephalosaurus* below and cross them out. Rearrange the remaining letters to find the other name this family of dinosaurs are sometimes called.

U E
A H N C B
S L A R E
A Y C O
U D P E C P
O S S H H

_ _ _ _ _ _ _ _ _

CERATOPSIANS

This group of herbivorous dinosaurs lived during the Cretaceous Period. They had stocky bodies and sharp beaks for cropping leaves and are famous for their elaborate head ornaments. Not all ceratopsians had a bony frill, horn, and spikes, but most had at least some kind of decoration. A few species walked on two legs, but most were four-legged.

WHICH IS WHICH?

Draw lines through the maze to match each of these ceratopsians to its description. Write the letters on the dotted lines once you've found them.

How to spot a ceratopsian

These herbivores came in a range of sizes. Here are some of their key features:

An enormous head
Ceratopsian heads were large compared to their body size.

A parrotlike beak
The upper part of the mouth had a sharp bone for slicing tough plants.

Skull ornaments
Each species had its own unique style of neck frill, spikes, or horns.

Four sturdy legs
Most ceratopsians walked on four sturdy legs, apart from a few bipedal species.

Thick, heavy bodies
Think rhinoceros or elephant and imagine a stampeding herd!

Psittacosaurus
(si-tak-a-SORE-us)
This dinosaur was smaller than many ceratopsians, but it had a larger-than-average brain.

Udanoceratops
(OO-dan-oh-SERRA-tops)
This unusual ceratopsian had a small neck frill and no face horns at all, but a pronounced beak.

Kosmoceratops
(KOS-moe-SERRA-tops)
With 15 horns and spikes on its face and frill, this was probably the most decorated ceratopsian.

Chasmosaurus
(KAZ-moe-SORE-us)
This ceratopsian had possibly the biggest head frill of all. It extended up and over its shoulders.

FIND THE CERATOPSIANS

More than 60 species of ceratopsian have been identified so far. Search the grid below for the names of seven of them hidden there.

S	T	Y	R	A	C	O	S	A	U	R	U	S	T	O	R
P	A	R	A	F	E	T	A	U	R	A	P	S	E	P	I
P	S	I	T	T	A	C	O	S	A	U	R	U	S	E	A
T	E	U	A	R	T	O	F	E	H	S	O	E	R	N	T
S	D	A	N	A	R	E	S	I	G	O	T	H	A	T	A
P	A	F	T	E	I	O	B	N	A	C	O	S	S	A	P
O	S	A	E	R	C	S	P	I	T	A	C	L	M	C	O
T	A	H	A	E	E	M	A	O	T	J	E	A	A	E	S
G	E	C	M	A	R	A	T	S	A	L	R	I	B	R	V
A	W	O	T	S	A	H	E	A	V	T	A	O	S	A	E
M	A	A	A	A	T	L	A	U	P	E	T	A	H	T	B
A	U	D	A	N	O	C	E	R	A	T	O	P	S	O	A
S	O	B	A	E	P	G	A	U	Z	A	P	V	O	P	S
W	E	N	O	B	S	E	R	S	C	N	S	A	U	S	A

Psittacosaurus   **Protoceratops**

Pentaceratops   **Udanoceratops**

Einiosaurus   **Triceratops**   **Styracosaurus**

COLOR THE FRILLS AND HORNS

Scientists think that ceratopsians recognized each other by their unique and colorful frills and horns. Use the key to color this *Pentaceratops*'s head.

Coloring key
1   2
3   4

COLOR IT!

IS IT A CERATOPSIAN?

Look at these three Cretaceous dinosaurs and answer the first two questions beneath each picture to decide whether it's a ceratopsian. Then add a check or a cross beside the last question. The information on these pages will help you.

CHECK IT!

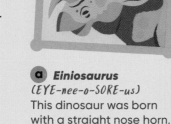

a *Einiosaurus*
(EYE-nee-o-SORE-us)
This dinosaur was born with a straight nose horn, which grew curved later.

☐ Does it have a frill?
☐ Does it have spikes?
☐ Is it a ceratopsian?

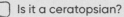

b *Carnotaurus*
(car-noe-TOR-us)
This dinosaur had sharp teeth, puny arms, and walked on two legs.

☐ Does it have a frill?
☐ Does it have a beak?
☐ Is it a ceratopsian?

c *Styracosaurus*
(sty-RACK-oh-SORE-us)
These dinosaurs probably grew their long frill spikes for display.

☐ Does it have a horn?
☐ Does it have a beak?
☐ Is it a ceratopsian?

SPOTLIGHT ON:
TRICERATOPS

With spectacular horns and a large neck frill, *Triceratops* was one of the largest ceratopsians of all time. It was also one of the last—surviving until the end of the Mesozoic Era, when most dinosaurs became extinct. *Triceratops*'s horn and frill weren't just ornaments—they were useful for fighting predators, such as *T. rex*, as well as other rival *Triceratops*.

Bony frill
Triceratops's impressive head frill was made of solid bone, covered in scaly skin.

TRICERATOPS

When: 71-66 mya (Late Cretaceous)
Habitat: Wooded plains
Length: 29.5 feet (9 m)
Diet: Low-growing plants
Pronunciation: try-SERRA-tops

As the animal got older, these bony bumps were absorbed into the frill.

COLOR IT!

The strong, sharp horns could grow up to 4 feet (1.3 m) long.

DECORATE ME!
With a skull that could grow to 8 feet (2.4 m) long, *Triceratops* had one of the largest heads of any land animal ever. Color its incredible frill, using the image in the box above to help you.

DRAW THE HORNS

Triceratops skulls and horns grew longer and changed shape as they got older. Read the descriptions under the heads, then draw the missing brow horns on this baby, juvenile, and adult.

DRAW IT!

One year old
Baby *Triceratops* had heads about 11 in (30 cm) long with short, stubby horns.

Older juvenile
As they matured, the brow horns grew longer, curved backward, and were about a third of the head length.

Adult
By full maturity, *Triceratops* horns were straight, pointed forward, and measured about half the length of the head.

Triceratops fossils show that its skin was covered in scales.

TRICERATOPS MEANS "THREE-HORNED FACE."

Triceratops walked on four legs, which helped spread out its sizable weight.

QUIZ YOURSELF!

Use what you have learned about *Triceratops* to take this quiz.

a What food did *Triceratops* like to eat?

....

b True or false: *Triceratops* was one of the largest ceratopsians.

....

c What type of skin covering did *Triceratops* have: scales or feathers?

....

d What does the name *Triceratops* mean?

....

e What shape were the horns of the older juvenile *Triceratops*?

....

FLYING REPTILES

Pterosaurs (*TEH-roe-sores*) first appeared during the Triassic Period, around the same time as the first dinosaurs. These reptiles were the first vertebrates to fly by flapping their wings. Unlike some dinosaurs, which evolved feathered wings, pterosaur wings were made from stretched skin.

SPOT THE SHADOWS
Pterosaurs overhead! Can you work out which one of these shadows is cast by which pterosaur? Check the cards below for help.

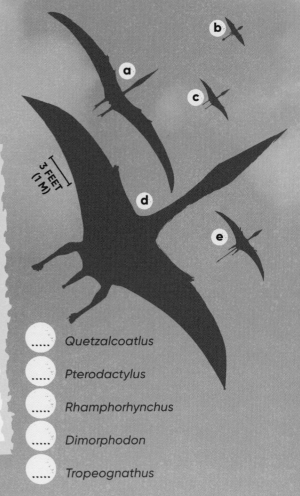

3 FEET (1 M)

..... Quetzalcoatlus

..... Pterodactylus

..... Rhamphorhynchus

..... Dimorphodon

..... Tropeognathus

The pterosaurs
Early pterosaurs were small, with long tails and short necks. Later species were larger, with short tails, long necks, and beaklike jaws, and some species had head crests. All pterosaurs had some features in common:

 Their wings were formed from skin stretched between the legs and extra-long finger bones.

 They flapped their wings to fly rather than gliding.

 Their bones were hollow, which made them light.

Their large eyes gave them excellent vision.

FILL IN THE FACTS
Use the word box below to fill in the missing facts about these amazing pterosaurs.

WRITE IT!

(Troh-PEE-og-NATH-us)

Jurassic   33 feet (10 m)

Carnivore

5 feet (1.5 m)   Europe

QUETZALCOATLUS
(KWETS-ul-coe-AT-lus)

This enormous pterosaur had the biggest wingspan of them all. It hunted for animals, including dinosaurs.

WINGSPAN: ....

DIET: Carnivore

WHEN: Cretaceous

WHERE: North America

PTERODACTYLUS
(TEH-roe-DACK-till-us)

This small pterosaur could fold its wings and walk on its hands and feet. Its name means "winged finger."

WINGSPAN: ....

DIET: Carnivore

WHEN: ....

WHERE: Europe

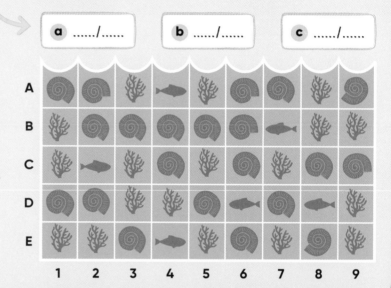

WRITE IT!

GO FISHING

Rhamphorhynchus was skilled at fishing. It soared over Jurassic oceans before diving headlong into the water to snatch up fish. There are six fish in this ocean for *Rhamphorhynchus* to try its luck. Find the three fish that have four shells and four plants in the surrounding squares, then write their coordinates in the spaces given above. Hint: Diagonal squares count, too.

a ...../.....   b ...../.....   c ...../.....

	1	2	3	4	5	6	7	8	9
A	shell	shell	plant	fish	plant	shell	shell	plant	shell
B	plant	shell	shell	shell	shell	shell	fish	plant	plant
C	plant	fish	plant	plant	shell	shell	shell	shell	shell
D	shell	shell	plant	plant	shell	fish	shell	fish	plant
E	plant	plant	shell	fish	plant	shell	plant	shell	shell

RHAMPHORHYNCHUS
(ram-foe-RINK-us)

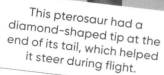

This pterosaur had a diamond-shaped tip at the end of its tail, which helped it steer during flight.

WINGSPAN: 6 feet (2 m)
DIET: ....
WHEN: Jurassic
WHERE: Europe

DIMORPHODON
(die-MOR-foe-don)

This pterosaur had an outsized head that took up a third of its small body length.

WINGSPAN: 3 feet (1 m)
DIET: Carnivore
WHEN: Jurassic
WHERE: ....

TROPEOGNATHUS
....

This large pterosaur had a big bump at the tip of its beak.

WINGSPAN: 20 feet (6 m)
DIET: Carnivore
WHEN: Jurassic
WHERE: South America

Types of marine reptiles

Many different groups of reptiles evolved to live in prehistoric waters at the time of the dinosaurs. Here are three of them:

Ichthyosaurs
(ICK-thee-oh-sores)
These air-breathing reptiles looked a little like dolphins. They were the first Mesozoic sea animals to reach enormous sizes.

Plesiosaurs
(PLEE-see-oh-sores)
There were two groups of plesiosaurs. Long-necked plesiosaurs had hugely elongated necks, with tiny heads. Pliosaurs, or short-necked plesiosaurs, had massive heads and jaws full of teeth.

Mosasaurs
(MOES-ah-sores)
These massive lizard relatives powered through the water with paddlelike limbs. They were mighty predators, with large jaws and many teeth.

MARINE REPTILES

Dinosaurs never lived fully in water, but prehistoric waters were home to plenty of other reptiles. Marine reptiles are ones that live in the sea. Some of them were large predators, which would have happily preyed on any dinosaurs that ventured too close to the water.

WHICH REPTILE?
Use the information on the left to help you work out which group each of these marine reptiles belongs to, then write the names in the spaces. Hint: Two of them are from the same group.

Ichthyosaur	Plesiosaur	Mosasaur

WRITE IT!

ELASMOSAURUS

a ....

MOSASAURUS

b ....

TEMNODONTOSAURUS

c ....

TYLOSAURUS

d ....

DIVIDE THE SCENE

One of the largest pliosaurs ever was called *Liopleurodon* (*LIE-oh-PLOOR-oh-don*), which hunted long-necked plesiosaurs. Can you draw two lines to divide this undersea scene into sections with one *Liopleurodon*, one plesiosaur, and six fish. Use a ruler to avoid cutting any fish in half!

THE LARGEST MOSASAUR SKELETON EVER FOUND IS 43 FEET (13 M) LONG!

WHO ELSE WAS THERE?

Other marine animals swam in Mesozoic seas, too. They weren't as big as the plesiosaurs or mosasaurs, but they were larger than their modern-day relatives. Connect the dots to reveal a marine reptile that was around at the time of the dinosaurs. The divers are for scale.

DRAW IT!

DECODE THE NAME

Replace each number below with its corresponding letter in the alphabet to reveal the name of this marine creature. (1 = a, 2 = b, 3 = c, and so on)

1 – 18 – 3 – 8 – 5 – 12 – 15 – 14

_ _ _ _ _ _ _ _

WHO SURVIVED?

All large land animals became extinct. Some species were able to survive—small animals and those that could hide from the devastation.

1. Put a cross by the animals in the scene below that became extinct and a check by the ones that survived.

2. Draw the animals that became extinct in these spaces, and write their names on the lines beneath.

DRAW IT!

☐ ANKYLOSAUR

☐ THEROPOD

☐ FROG

☐ SNAKE

☐ MAMMAL

☐ ORNITHOPOD

THE LAST DAY OF THE CRETACEOUS

Around 66 million years ago, an enormous asteroid flew through Earth's atmosphere and into our planet. It caused a mass extinction event, wiping out around 70 percent of all plant and animal species. On land, no animal bigger than a dog survived the asteroid's impact, and Earth's climate was radically altered.

A deathly impact
The asteroid vaporized as it hit Earth, in a catastrophic explosion that killed everything in the nearby area. The impact triggered geological events all across the planet, such as volcanic eruptions and earthquakes, and ash and smoke blocked the Sun.

NAME THAT ROCK

What is the name of the space rock that collided with Earth?

D E T A S O I R

_ _ _ _ _ _ _ _

THE SPACE ROCK THAT KILLED THE DINOSAURS WAS AROUND **6 MILES** (10 KM) WIDE.

☐ BIRD

☐ PTEROSAUR

☐ FISH

☐ TURTLE

☐ SAUROPOD

WHAT HAPPENED AFTERWARD?

These images show what happened to the planet in the aftermath of the asteroid impact. The pictures are jumbled. Draw a line to match each one to the correct description.

MATCH IT!

1 Intense heat
Friction from falling debris raises temperatures across the planet. Forests burn. Most dinosaurs perish.

2 Cold and dark
Dust and soot block the Sun, creating a three-year "impact winter." Birds eat seeds to survive.

3 Plants regrow
About 100,000 years after impact, forests start to rebuild gradually. There is an explosion of ferns.

4 Age of mammals
A million years later, surviving species—such as mammals—have begun to evolve to occupy the land.

a

b

c

d

AFTER THE DINOSAURS

With the dinosaurs gone, other animals began to fill niches they had left behind. Mammals that survived the extinction evolved into new shapes and sizes. The Mesozoic Era of the dinosaurs had ended and a new era had begun—the Cenozoic, known as "The Age of Mammals."

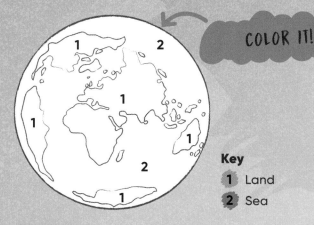

COLOR IT!

Key
1 Land
2 Sea

The Cenozoic Era
Earth was cooler in the Cenozoic than the Mesozoic, and there were several ice ages. Flowering plants flourished. Insects, reptiles, and other animals all evolved to survive.

ADD THE NAMES
Read about six of the animals featured in the timeline below. Work out which animal each description is talking about and add the correct name.

a ....
This huge ground sloth evolved around 200,000 years before modern humans. It stood on its hind legs to nibble leaves.

b ....
As herbivores grew bigger, so did predators. This massive land mammal had hooves like a hippo and a snout like a giant wolf.

c ....
This rhinolike animal evolved around 55.8 million years ago (mya) to fill the space left by the herbivorous dinosaurs.

d ....
These dinosaurs survived the extinction at the end of the Cretaceous. Some evolved into huge, flightless species.

e ....
This fierce, saber-toothed cat was an expert hunter. It could bring down herbivores bigger than itself.

f ....
These hairy, elephantlike mammals evolved around 200,000 years ago and grazed on grass and leaves.

DINOSAURS

A massive asteroid hit Earth.

66 MYA

55.8 MYA

45 MYA

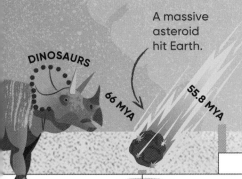

MORE THAN **99%** OF ALL SPECIES THAT HAVE EVER LIVED ON EARTH ARE NOW **EXTINCT!**

ANDREWSARCHUS

UINTATHERIUM

BIRDS

COIL THE SNAKES

Snakes grew larger and heavier after the dinosaurs became extinct. *Titanoboa* was the longest and heaviest snake ever to exist. Can you fit the world's longest modern snakes and *Titanoboa* into this grid? The "X"s indicate empty squares.

DRAW IT!

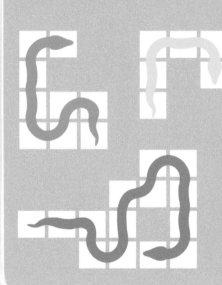

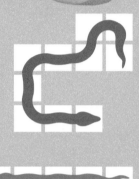
TITANOBOA

Key

King cobra
18 feet (5.5 m)
5 squares

Reticulated python
33 feet (10 m)
10 squares

Green anaconda
29 feet (9 m)
9 squares

Titanoboa
48 feet (14.6 m)
14 squares

Indian python
21 feet (6.4 m)
6 squares

WHO LIVED WHEN?

The timeline below shows some of the animals that lived after the dinosaurs. Use the key to color when each animal lived.

Coloring key

- Dinosaurs
- Birds
- *Uintatherium*
- *Andrewsarchus*
- *Smilodon*
- Mammoth
- *Megatherium*
- Humans

1 MYA

400,000 YEARS AGO (YA)

200,000 YA

8,000 YA

4,000 YA

PRESENT DAY

SMILODON

MEGATHERIUM

MAMMOTH

MODERN HUMANS

From dinosaur to bird

Most modern birds have flight feathers, short tails, and curved breast bones that have strong muscles attached to them, allowing flight. These features took tens of millions of years to evolve.

Velociraptor
(vel-OSS-ee-RAP-tor)
The theropod ancestors of birds had wings and feathers but were unable to fly.

Archaeopteryx
(ar-kee-OP-ter-icks)
The earliest birds were probably able to glide through the air or flap for short distances.

Magpie goose
Some of today's birds are able to fly for thousands of miles without stopping.

MODERN DINOSAURS

The dinosaurs didn't die out completely. A handful of two-legged, feathered theropods appear to have survived the extinction event at the end of the Cretaceous Period. Over time, they evolved, changing little by little, until they became the birds we see around us today.

MATCH THE BEHAVIORS

Scientists study how birds behave to help them try to work out what the dinosaurs would have done. Here are some behaviors probably shared by dinosaurs. Match each picture to the correct description.

a ....

c ....

WRITE IT!

b ....

Hunting
Eagles pin down their prey with sharp talons, then rip it apart with their beaks.

Nesting
Seabirds, such as puffins, build their nests close together in colonies and share guard duty.

Care for young
Many birds, such as chickens, take care of their young once they have hatched from their eggs.

DRAW MODERN DINOSAURS

Here are some things that birds share with the dinosaurs they evolved from. The small circles show dinosaur features. Draw pictures of modern birds doing the things mentioned underneath.

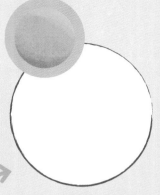

DRAW IT!

Eggs
Birds lay eggs, and so did dinosaurs. Some dinos sat on their eggs to keep them warm, like birds do. Draw a bird sitting on its eggs.

Feathers
Fossils show us that many dinosaurs had feathers. All birds have feathers, although some can't fly. Draw a bird in flight.

Scaly feet
Birds have scaly feet, with a claw at the end of each toe, just like dinosaurs did. Draw a bird perched on a tree, gripping the branch.

DESIGN THE DISPLAY

Modern birds use their feathers to show off their health and skills to attract a mate. A peacock's tail is one of the best examples. It is likely that some dinosaurs also used their feathers for display. Color this peacock's tail, plus the wing and tail feathers of *Caudipteryx* (*caw-DIP-ter-icks*), a dinosaur from the Cretaceous Period.

THE FIRST **BIRDS** HAD **TEETH** INSIDE THEIR MOUTHS.

COLOR IT!

DINOSAUR QUIZ

Now it's time to test how much you've learned about dinosaurs by taking this quiz. You can go back through earlier pages to look for clues and check up on some of the facts, if you need to. Good luck!

HOW DID YOU DO?

Once you have answered the questions, you can check your answers at the back of the book. How many did you get right?

12-17 Dinosaur expert extraordinaire!

6-11 You could probably identify a *Triceratops*.

0-5 You couldn't tell a *Spinosaurus* from a sausage.

1 Which group of dinosaurs had long necks and large, pillarlike legs?

....

2 Footprints are a type of trace fossil.

☐ True   ☐ False

3 What is the name for the study of prehistoric life?

a Geology
b Paleontology
c Biology
d Seismology

4 Which of these body parts were used for defense? You can choose more than one.

a Horns
b Armor
c Nostrils
d Spikes

5 What is the name for a fossilized poop?

a A poorolite
b A dungalite
c A dirtalite
d A coprolite

6 Which group of dinosaurs had two rows of bony plates running along their backs?

....

7 Which geological era did the dinosaurs exist in?

- **a** The Mesozoic
- **b** The Paleozoic
- **c** The Metrozoic
- **d** The Cenozoic

8 All dinosaurs were carnivores.

☐ True ☐ False

9 Which of these Jurassic creatures is a pterosaur?

a
b
c
d

10 Which time period came after the Jurassic?

- **a** The Tenacious
- **b** The Audacious
- **c** The Cretaceous
- **d** The Vivacious

11 Which large, elephantlike mammal appeared after the dinosaur extinction?

- **a** Hairy human
- **b** Cotton mammal
- **c** Hessian oliphant
- **d** Woolly mammoth

12 Which large theropod is likely to have spent time hunting for fish?

....

13 Birds are theropods.

☐ True ☐ False

14 What caused the dinosaur extinction?

- **a** Dinosaur farts
- **b** An asteroid impact
- **c** Too many males
- **d** Aliens

15 Do you remember the name of this thick-headed lizard?

....

16 Name these three types of marine reptiles:

a ....

b ....

c ....

DINORAMA!

Here is a glimpse into life in Late Cretaceous North America. Herbivores graze, carnivores hunt, and water brings them all together. Color in the picture, then draw some things you see in the panel on the right.

COLOR IT!

WHAT DO YOU SEE?
Find the five things listed below and draw them in the boxes.

DRAW IT!

A Triceratops

A Tyrannosaurus rex

A sauropod

An ancient crocodile

A pterosaur

ROAR-SOME PREHISTORIC FACTS

Some Mesozoic creatures were big, and others small; some were fast, and others slow. Here are a few more facts about these roar-some animals.

THE LENGTH OF THE LONGEST KNOWN DINOSAUR HORN

4 FEET (1.2 M)

THE NUMBER OF YEARS THE AGE OF DINOSAURS LASTED FOR

177 MILLION

THE NUMBER OF KNOWN DINOSAUR SPECIES (SO FAR)

MORE THAN 1,000

THE SHOULDER HEIGHT OF THE TITANOSAUR DREADNOUGHTUS

28 FEET (8.5 M)

THE LENGTH OF THE TAIL SPIKES ON A STEGOSAURUS

3.3 FEET (1 M)

What's for dinner?
It is estimated that 65 percent of dinosaurs were plant-eating herbivores. That means only 35 percent were meat-eating carnivores.

 Carnivores
These dinosaurs ate insects, mammals, and even other dinosaurs.

Herbivores
These dinosaurs ate leaves, seeds, and berries.

Fastest predators
The fastest dinosaurs were often carnivores. Here are a few of them and the speeds they are thought to have reached, plus today's fastest land predator, the cheetah.

11 MPH (18 KPH)
Compsognathus

22 MPH (36 KPH)
Velociraptor

28 MPH (45 KPH)
Ornithomimus

34 MPH (54 KPH)
Allosaurus

34 MPH (54 KPH)
Megalosaurus

75 MPH (120 KPH)
Cheetah

Biggest, smallest, longest ...

Prehistoric creatures came in a huge range of shapes and sizes, and they followed as many different lifestyles as animals do today. Here are a few facts about some incredible fossils that have been discovered.

Smallest lizard in amber
A tiny lizard, just 1.4 in (3.5 cm) long, was found fossilized in tree sap from 110 million years ago.

Biggest dinosaur eggs
The longest fossilized dinosaur eggs are 2 feet (60 cm) long and date from the Cretaceous Period.

Biggest dinosaur brain
Troodon had the biggest dinosaur brain compared to body size. It may have been as clever as modern birds.

Longest claws
The longest dinosaur claws were 3 feet (91 cm) long and belonged to *Therizinosaurus*.

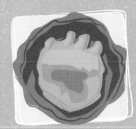

Biggest dinosaur skull
This award goes to *Pentaceratops*, whose skull could grow up to 10 feet (3.2 m) long.

Strongest bite
As if *T. rex* wasn't scary enough, it could exert a bone-crushing bite force of 6.4 tons (5.8 tonnes).

Largest footprint
In 2017, the tracks of a sauropod with 5.75-feet (1.75-m) long footprints were found in Australia.

Smallest dinosaur
The smallest dinosaur discovered to date is a tiny, feathered theropod named *Microraptor*.

Super sizes

Some of the dinosaurs and prehistoric animals that lived alongside them reached gigantic sizes. Here are a handful of examples, with a human for you to compare them to.

Biggest herbivore
Argentinosaurus
96 tons (88 tonnes)

Biggest carnivore
Spinosaurus
8.2 tons (7.4 tonnes)

Modern human adult
154 lb (70 kg)

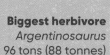

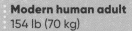

Biggest flying reptile
Quetzalcoatlus
550 lb (240 kg)

Biggest marine reptile
Shastasaurus
71 tons (64 tonnes)

GLOSSARY

Amber
Sticky resin that has oozed from a tree and become hardened over many millions of years.

Ammonite
A marine mollusk with a coiled shell and octopuslike tentacles that was common in the Mesozoic Era.

Anatomy
A branch of science involving the study of the physical structure and internal workings of all living things.

Ancestor
An animal or plant species from which a more recent species has evolved.

Ankylosaur
One of the main types of ornithischian dinosaur, which had a body covered in bony armor.

Armor
Naturally hard body covering that provides protection for an animal.

Arthropod
An invertebrate with a segmented body and a hard outer covering called an exoskeleton. Living examples of arthropods include insects and spiders.

Bipedal
Walking on two legs.

Birds
The only living dinosaurs. They evolved from bipedal theropods, such as *T. rex*, and survived the end-Cretaceous mass extinction.

Breeding
Males and females coming together to produce eggs and/or young.

Brooding
Adult animals keeping eggs or hatchlings warm by covering them with their bodies or wings.

Camouflage
Colors or patterns on an animal's skin, fur, or feathers that help it blend in with its environment.

Carnivore
An animal that eats meat.

Cenozoic Era
The era that followed the age of the dinosaurs, from 66 million years ago to the present day.

Ceratopsian
One of a group of horned dinosaurs, which usually had horns on its face and a bony frill over its neck.

Coprolite
Fossilized animal poop.

Crest
A growth on the head of an animal, likely used for display.

Cretaceous Period
The third period of the Mesozoic Era, which began 145 million years ago and ended 66 million years ago.

Cycad
A type of tropical plant that has a broad crown of leaves and looks like—but is not related to—palm trees.

Dinosaur
One of a group of archosaurs with upright limbs that dominated life on land during the Mesozoic Era.

Display
A demonstration of fitness or strength, designed to impress a mate or intimidate a rival.

Diversification
The evolutionary changes in a species that lead to the formation of a new species.

Environment
The surroundings of a living thing.

Era
A long span of geological time, such as the Mesozoic, that marks a particular division in the history of life. Eras are often made up of several shorter divisions of time, called periods.

Evolution
The process by which living things change over time.

Evolve
To change over time.

Excavation
The process of carefully digging out a fossil from rock.

Extinct
Having died out completely. An extinct species has no living individuals.

Flowering plant
A plant that produces flowers and fruits.

Fossil
The remains or traces of any living thing that survive the normal process of decay and are often preserved by being turned to stone.

Fossilization
Process by which an animal or plant becomes a fossil.

Frill
A bony, platelike extension around the neck of an animal.

Habitat
The natural home environment of an animal or plant.

Herbivore
An animal that eats plants.

Ichthyosaur
One of a group of dolphinlike marine reptiles that was very successful in the early Mesozoic Era.

Impression
The mark or outline left by an object or animal on a soft surface.

Incubate
To keep eggs warm so they develop and hatch.

Invertebrate
An animal without a vertebral column (backbone).

Jurassic Period
The second of three periods making up the Mesozoic Era, from 201 to 145 million years ago.

Mammals
Warm-blooded vertebrate animals that have skin covered in hair and feed their young milk.

Marine
To do with the ocean or sea.

Marine reptile
A reptile that lives in the sea, but also used to refer to the plesiosaurs, ichthyosaurs, and similar groups that became extinct at the end of the Mesozoic Era.

Mass extinction
A disaster that causes the disappearance of many types of life forms.

Mesozoic Era
The era known as the age of the dinosaurs, from 252 to 66 million years ago.

Meteorite
A piece of rock from space that enters Earth's atmosphere and reaches the ground without burning up.

Omnivore
An animal that eats both plants and animals.

Ornithischian
One of the two main divisions of dinosaurs. Ornithischians were "bird-hipped" and mostly herbivores. Some were omnivores.

Ornithopod
One of a group of plant-eating dinosaurs that were very successful, especially in the Cretaceous Period.

Pachycephalosaur
One of a group of plant-eating or omnivorous dinosaurs with two legs and domed skulls. They lived in the Cretaceous Period.

Paleontologist
A scientist who specializes in the study of fossils.

Paleontology
The study of fossils.

Paleozoic Era
The era that came before the Mesozoic Era. It lasted from 542 to 252 million years ago.

Plesiosaur
Type of marine reptile that usually had a long neck, alive in the Mesozoic Era.

Predator
An animal that kills other animals for food.

Prehistoric
The time before information was written down or documented.

Preserved
Not decayed or been damaged much over time.

Prey
An animal that is eaten by another animal.

Pterosaur
One of a group of flying reptiles that lived during the Mesozoic Era, with wings of complex skin that were each supported by the bones of a single long finger.

Reptiles
Cold-blooded animals with scaly skin that reproduce by laying eggs. This group includes snakes, lizards, crocodiles, flying reptiles, marine reptiles, and dinosaurs.

Saurischian
One of the two main divisions of dinosaurs that typically had "lizardlike" hips.

Sauropod
One of a group of long-necked, plant-eating dinosaurs.

Scavenger
An animal that eats the remains of dead animals.

Serrated
Saw-toothed, like a bread knife.

Species
A group of individual living things that can interbreed successfully.

Stegosaur
One of a group of armored dinosaurs with large plates and spines on their backs.

Theropod
One of a group of saurischian dinosaurs that were bipedal and usually meat-eaters.

Trace fossil
The fossilized remains of prehistoric creatures' activities rather than their bodies. Trace fossils include footprints, droppings, or egg shells.

Triassic Period
The first period of the Mesozoic Era, from 252 to 201 million years ago.

Trilobite
A kind of extinct arthropod with a body divided into three sections.

Vertebrate
Animal with a vertebral column (backbone).

Warm-blooded
An animal that maintains a constant internal body temperature. It is likely that dinosaurs were warm-blooded.

ANSWERS

4-5 WHAT IS A DINOSAUR?

MATCH THE CREATURES!
a Crocodylomorphs
b Pterosaurs
c Ichthyosaurs
d Plesiosaurs

WHOSE LEGS?
a Lizard
b Crocodile
c Dinosaur

IS IT A DINOSAUR?
Pterodactylus—No
Hypsilophodon—Yes
Deinosuchus—No
Sauroposeidon—Yes
Stenopterygius—No
Archelon—No

6-7 PALEONTOLOGY

COMPLETE THE SKELETON

STUDY THE BONES
a Two
b Long and sharp
c Other dinosaurs

NAME THAT DINOSAUR
a Spiked lizard
b Three-horned face
c Heavy claw
d Chicken mimic
e Parrot lizard

8-9 DIGGING UP DINOSAURS

DRAW THE TOOLS
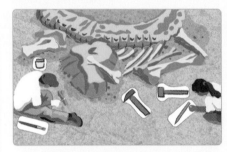

LOCATE THE FOSSILS
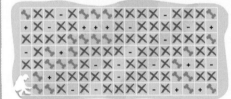

10-11 HOW DO FOSSILS FORM?

FIND THE FOSSIL NAME
Ammonite

BURY THE DINO BONES
Here's what ours looks like!

WHAT WENT WRONG?
a Nothing left
b No sediment
c Ocean waves

12-13 FOSSILS

TRAP THE CREATURES

WHICH TYPE?
a Cast
b Trace
c Body
d Mold
e Trace
f Body

14-15 GEOLOGICAL TIMELINE

COLOR THE TIMELINE

FIND THE CREATURES
a

Pterygotus

b
Lystrosaurus

c
Sauroposeidon

NAME THAT ERA
Mesozoic Era

16-17 THE TRIASSIC PERIOD

TRIASSIC EARTH

DRAW THE ANIMALS

UNSCRAMBLE THE CREATURE
Cockroach

WHO CAME FIRST?
1. *Herrerasaurus*
2. *Coelophysis*
3. *Plateosaurus*

18-19 THE JURASSIC PERIOD

JURASSIC EARTH

COMPLETE THE PROFILES
Heterodontosaurus
When: 200–190 mya

Cryolophosaurus
Type: Theropod

Archaeopteryx
Length: 1.5 feet (45 cm)

Scelidosaurus
Diet: Plants

Diplodocus
Habitat: Plains with trees

FOLLOW THE PTEROSAURS
Pterodactylus
Dearc Sgiathanach

WHAT'S ITS NAME?
The Jurassic

DRAW THE FOREST
Here's what ours looks like!

20-21 THE CRETACEOUS PERIOD

CRETACEOUS EARTH

COMPLETE THE DINOSAUR SCENE

WHO AM I?
Muttaburrasaurus

BONUS QUESTION
Adelolophus

22-23 PREHISTORIC PLANTS

WHICH TYPE OF PLANT?
a Fern
b Flowering plant
c Horsetail

GUIDE THE BEETLE

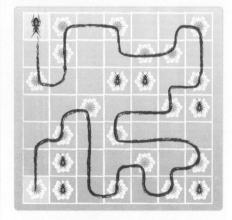

DRAW THE GINKGO

24-25 BODY BASICS

INVENT A DINOSAUR
Here's what ours looks like!

SCALES OR FEATHERS?
- **a** Psittacosaurus
- **b** Edmontosaurus
- **c** Sinosauropteryx

FIND THE NEST

26-27 WHAT DID THEY EAT?

HERBIVORE OR CARNIVORE?
Iguanodon—Herbivore
Spinosaurus—Carnivore
Styracosaurus—Herbivore
Carcharodontosaurus—Carnivore
Corythosaurus—Herbivore

WHAT'S FOR DINNER?

WHO EATS EVERYTHING?
Omnivore

28-29 WALKING WITH DINOSAURS

COLOR THE PATHS

REVEAL THE PRINTS

 a Sauropod

 b Theropod

 c Ornithopod

WHO GOES THERE?
- **a** Sauropod
- **b** Theropod
- **c** Ornithopod

30-31 HUNTING

WHO'S FOR DINNER?
Coelurus

GUIDE THE HUNTERS TO THEIR PREY

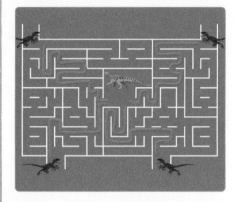

NAME THE SCROUNGERS
Scavengers

32-33 DINOSAUR DEFENSES

IDENTIFY EACH DINOSAUR
- **a** Styracosaurus
- **b** Stegosaurus
- **c** Triceratops
- **d** Edmontonia
- **e** Barosaurus
- **f** Iguanodon

WHAT'S MY WEAPON?

CREATE A SUPER-DINO
Here's what ours looks like!

34-35 FEATHERS

WHICH IS WHICH?

 a Bristle feather

 b Fluffy feather

 c Flight feather

 d Armored plates

COMPLETE THE WINGS

COLOR THE FEATHER

36-37 EGGS AND NESTS

MATCH THE PARTS
a Amniotic sac
b Eyes
c Shell
d Yolk
e Embryo

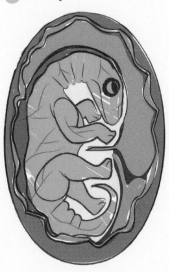

FILL THE NESTS

 Oviraptor

 Maiasaura

 Titanosaurus

WHICH ONE IS MY SHELL?

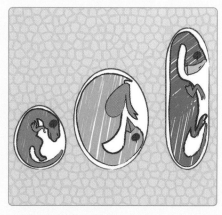

GUIDE THE MAIASAURA

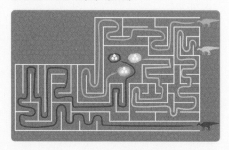

38-39 DINOSAUR GROUPS

COUNT THE DINOSAURS
Ornithopods

IDENTIFY THE HIPS

 a Ornithischian

 b Saurischian

WHICH GROUP?
Eodromaeus—Theropod
Diplodocus—Sauropod
Sauropelta—Ankylosaur
Parasaurolophus—Ornithopod
Acrotholus—Pachycephalosaur
Chialingosaurus—Stegosaur
Protoceratops—Ceratopsian

40-41 THEROPODS

FILL IN THE FACTS
Tyrannosaurus rex
Found in: USA

Baryonyx
Diet: Fish

Caudipteryx
When: Cretaceous

Ceratosaurus
Length: 20 feet (6 m)

Velociraptor
Weight: 33 lb (15 kg)

CAMOUFLAGE OR DISPLAY?
Here's what ours look like!

FIND THE LIVING THEROPODS
Birds

42-43 SPOTLIGHT ON: TYRANNOSAURUS REX

COMPLETE THE KILLING TEETH

WHY SUCH TINY ARMS?
Any theory might be true.

DRAW THE MIGHTY PREDATOR

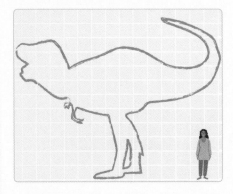

HUNT THE DINOS

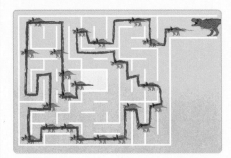

44-45 SPOTLIGHT ON: SPINOSAURUS

CATCH THE FISH

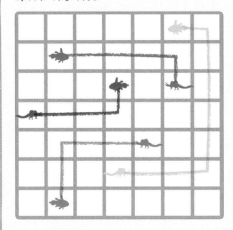

COLOR THE GIANT HUNTER
Here's what ours looks like!

46-47 SPOTLIGHT ON: VELOCIRAPTOR

HUNT WITH VELOCIRAPTOR
Here's what ours look like!

a   2 p.m.

b   7 p.m.

c   7:30 p.m.

d   7:45 p.m.

e   9 p.m.

f   5 a.m.

SEE THROUGH THEIR EYES

What *Protoceratops* saw

What *Zalambdalestes* saw

SPOT THE IMPOSTOR!

48-49 SAUROPODS

WHO AM I?

Name:
Giraffatitan

Country:
Tanzania

Length:
85 feet (26 m)

I like to eat:
Tree leaves

TRUE OR FALSE?

a True
b False (quite the opposite)
c True
d False (that's just silly!)

FIND THE EGGS
We found 18.

50-51 SPOTLIGHT ON: ARGENTINOSAURUS

DRAW A TITANO-HUMAN

BALANCE THE SCALES

SEARCH THE SKIN
Titanosaurs

52-53 STEGOSAURS

COMPLETE THE STEGOSAUR

FILL IN THE FACTS
Name:
Scutellosaurus

Where:
USA

When:
Early Jurassic

Length:
3 feet (1 m)

FIND THE IMPOSTORS

Huayangosaurus
Stegosaur

Triceratops
Not a stegosaur

Lexovisaurus
Stegosaur

Ankylosaurus
Not a stegosaur

Miragaia
Stegosaur

54-55 SPOTLIGHT ON: STEGOSAURUS

FIND THE FOOD
Here's what we found!

 Cycads

 Ferns

 Horsetails

COLOR THE PLATES

AVOID THE ALLOSAURUS!

USE YOUR BRAINPOWER

a Ostrich
b Elephant
c Human
d *Stegosaurus*

56-57 ANKYLOSAURS

WHICH ANKYLOSAUR IS WHICH?

a Gastonia

b Sauropelta

c Ankylosaurus

d Gargoyleosaurus

ADD THE ARMOR

WHAT TO EAT?

Fern—Yes

Fish—No

Meat—No

Seeds—Yes

UNSCRAMBLE THE NAMES

a Sauropelta

b Gargoyleosaurus

58-59 ORNITHOPODS

FILL IN THE FACTS

Iguanodon
Length: 30 feet (9 m)

Ouranosaurus
When: Early Cretaceous

Hypsilophodon
Length: 6 feet (2 m)

Maiasaura
(MY-a-SORE-ah)
Weight: 4.4 tons (4 tonnes)

CONNECT THE HERD

COMPLETE THE CRESTS

Here's what ours look like!

60-61 SPOTLIGHT ON: PARASAUROLOPHUS

FIND THE GROUP

Hadrosaurs

HOW DID PARASAUROLOPHUS CALL?

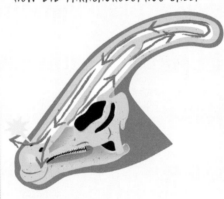

WARN THE HERD

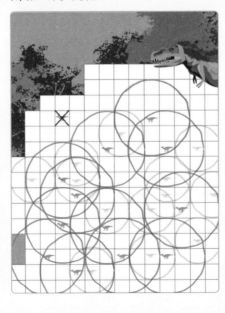

62-63 PACHYCEPHALOSAURS

REVEAL THE YOUNG ONE

COLOR ME IN!

Here's what ours looks like!

CLASH THE HEADS

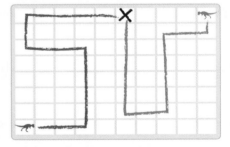

WHAT'S THEIR OTHER NAME?

Bone heads

64-65 CERATOPSIANS

WHICH IS WHICH?

a Psittacosaurus

b Udanoceratops

c Kosmoceratops

d Chasmosaurus

FIND THE CERATOPSIANS

S	T	Y	R	A	C	O	S	A	U	R	U	S		T	O	R			
P	A	R	A	F	E	T	A	U	R	A	P	S		E		P			I
P	S	I	T	T	A	C	O	S	A	U	R	U	S			E			A
T	E	U	A	R	T	O	F	E	H	S	O	E	R		N		T		P
S	D	A	N	A	R	E	S	I	G	O	T	H	S		S		A		O
P	A	F	T	E	I	O	B	N	A	C	O	S	S			C			S
O	S	A	E	R	C	S	P	I	T	A	C	L	M		E		R		V
T	A	H	A	E	E	M	A	T	S	A	L	R	I		A		A		E
G	E	C	M	A	R	A	T	S	A	L	R	I	B			R			B
A	W	O	T	S	A	H	E	A	V	T	A	O	S		S		T		A
M	A	A	A	A	T	L	A	U	P	E	T	A	H		T		S		S
A	U	D	A	N	O	C	E	R	A	T	O	P	S		O				
S	O	B	A	E	P	G	A	U	Z	A	P	V	O		P				
W	E	N	O	B	S	E	R	S	C	N	S	A	U						

COLOR THE FRILLS AND HORNS

IS IT A CERATOPSIAN?

- **a** Yes
- **b** No
- **c** Yes

66-67 SPOTLIGHT ON: TRICERATOPS

DECORATE ME!
Here's what ours looks like!

DRAW THE HORNS

One year old

Older juvenile

Adult

QUIZ YOURSELF!

- **a** Low-growing plants
- **b** True
- **c** Scales
- **d** Three-horned face
- **e** Curved backward

68-69 FLYING REPTILES

SPOT THE SHADOWS

- **a** Tropeognathus
- **b** Dimorphodon
- **c** Pterodactylus
- **d** Quetzalcoatlus
- **e** Rhamphorhynchus

FILL IN THE FACTS

Quetzalcoatlus
Wingspan: 33 feet (10 m)

Pterodactylus
Wingspan: 5 feet (1.5 m)
When: Jurassic

Rhamphorhynchus
Diet: Carnivore

Dimorphodon
Where: Europe

Tropeognathus
(Troh-PEE-og-NATH-us)

GO FISHING

- **a** 2, C
- **b** 6, D
- **c** 8, D

70-71 MARINE REPTILES

WHICH REPTILE?

- **a** Plesiosaur
- **b** Mosasaur
- **c** Ichthyosaur
- **d** Mosasaur

DIVIDE THE SCENE

WHO ELSE WAS THERE?

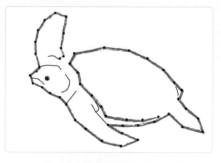

DECODE THE NAME
Archelon

72-73 THE LAST DAY OF THE CRETACEOUS

WHO SURVIVED?

- ☑ Snake
- ☒ Ankylosaur
- ☑ Frog
- ☒ Theropod
- ☑ Mammal
- ☒ Ornithopod
- ☒ Sauropod
- ☒ Pterosaur
- ☑ Fish
- ☑ Bird
- ☑ Turtle

 Ankylosaur

 Theropod

 Ornithopod

 Sauropod

 Pterosaur

NAME THAT ROCK
Asteroid

WHAT HAPPENED AFTERWARD?

1. b
2. d
3. c
4. a

74-75 AFTER THE DINOSAURS

THE CENOZOIC ERA

ADD THE NAMES

- a *Megatherium*
- b *Andrewsarchus*
- c *Uintatherium*
- d Birds
- e *Smilodon*
- f Mammoth

WHO LIVED WHEN?

COIL THE SNAKES

76-77 MODERN DINOSAURS

MATCH THE BEHAVIORS

- a Care for young
- b Hunting
- c Nesting

DRAW MODERN DINOSAURS
Here's what ours look like!

 Eggs

 Feathers

 Scaly feet

DESIGN THE DISPLAY

78-79 DINOSAUR QUIZ

1. Sauropods
2. True
3. b) Paleontology
4. a) Horns, b) Armor, d) Spikes
5. d) A coprolite
6. Stegosaurs
7. a) The Mesozoic
8. False (many of them were herbivores or omnivores)
9. c) *Pterodactylus*
10. c) The Cretaceous
11. d) Woolly mammoth
12. *Spinosaurus*
13. True
14. b) An asteroid impact
15. *Pachycephalosaurus*
16. a) Ichthyosaur
    b) Plesiosaur
    c) Mosasaur

WHAT DO YOU SEE?

A *Triceratops*

An ancient crocodile

A *Tyrannosaurus rex*

A sauropod

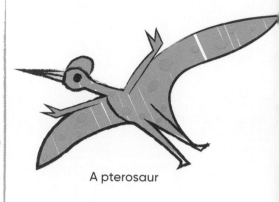

A pterosaur

COLOR YOUR OWN!
Here's what ours looks like!

INDEX

ACKNOWLEDGMENTS

DK would like to thank the following for their help with this book:
John Friend for proofreading; Elizabeth Wise for compiling the index;
Andrea Page for editorial assistance; Vacharin Vacharopast for visual
dinosaur consultancy; Gus Scott for additional illustrations; Laura Gardner
for additional jacket design.

The publisher would like to thank the following for
their kind permission to reproduce their photographs:

(Key: a-above; b-below/bottom; c-center; f-far; l-left; r-right; t-top)

12 123RF.com: picsfive (b/x4). **Dreamstime.com:** Bjrn Wylezich (tl).
13 123RF.com: alexeykonovalenko (cb). **Alamy Stock Photo:** Sabena
Jane Blackbird (crb); Chris Craggs (cl/x2). **Dorling Kindersley:**
Andy Crawford Courtesy of Dorset Dinosaur Museum (c).
Dreamstime.com: Jakekohlberg (cr). **22 Alamy Stock Photo:**
John Cancalosi (br); Natural History Museum, London (cb).
Dorling Kindersley: Gary Ombler / Oxford Museum of
Natural History (crb). **23 Dreamstime.com:** Dbalinda (bl).
25 Getty Images: Toronto Star / Bernard Weil (cra).
Shutterstock.com: Scott K. MacLeod (ca).

35 Dorling Kindersley: Colin Keates / Natural History Museum, London (tr).
42 Dorling Kindersley: Gary Ombler / Senckenberg Gesellschaft Fuer
Naturforschung Museum (tl). **46 Dorling Kindersley:** Dan Crisp (cr). **68 Dorling
Kindersley:** Roby Braun / Gary Ombler (c). **72 Science Photo Library:** D. Van
Ravenswaay (crb). **76 Dorling Kindersley:** Dan Crisp (tl); Frank Greenaway /
National Birds of Prey Centre, Gloucestershire (cb). **Dreamstime.com:** Elena
Elisseeva (cr); Omidiii (c)

All other images © Dorling Kindersley